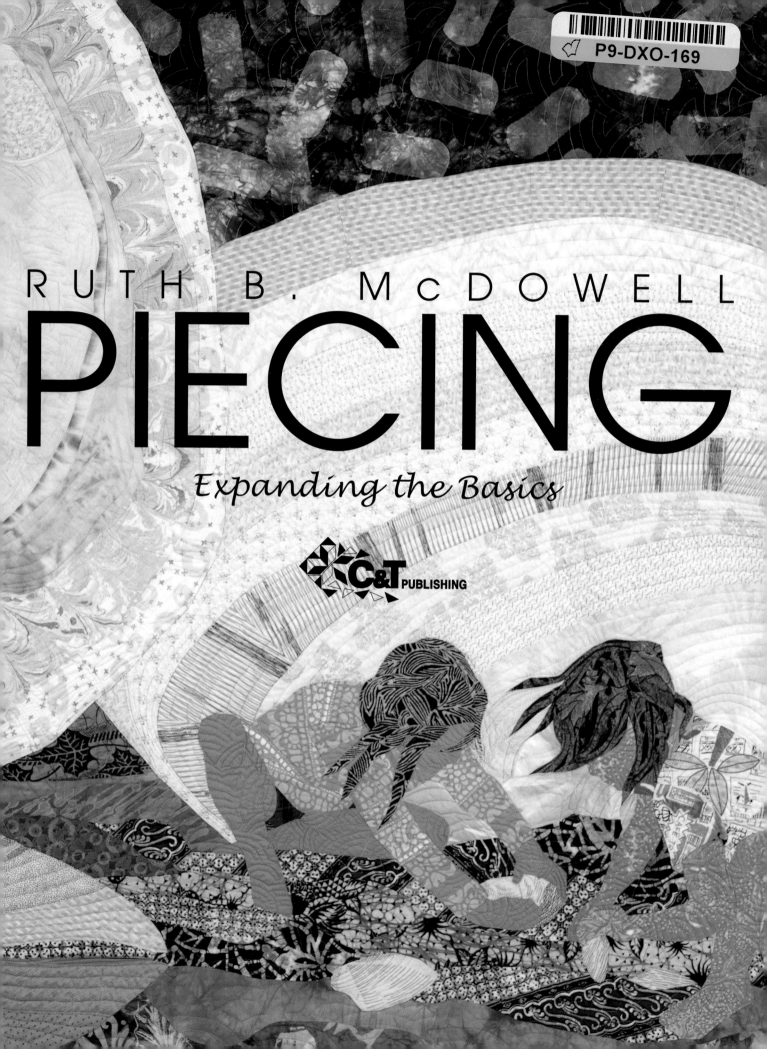

RUTH B. McDOWELL

PIECING

Expanding the Basics

C&T PUBLISHING

Developmental Editor: Barbara Konzak Kuhn
Technical Editor: Sally Loss Lanzarotti
Copy Editor: Emily McDowell
Book Design: John Cram
Cover Design: John Cram
Illustrator: Kandy Peterson
All photography by D. Caras unless otherwise noted.

Title page: Detail of *Blueprint for an Ancient Implement*, shown on page 13
Legal page: Detail of *Three Grizzly Bears*, shown on page 117
Preface page: Detail of *Maine Woods*, shown on page 154

Library of Congress Cataloging-in-Publication Data
McDowell, Ruth B.
    Piecing : expanding the basics / Ruth B. McDowell.
        p.   cm.
    Includes bibliographical references and index.
    ISBN 1-57120-041-X
    1. Patchwork quilts--Design.   2. Patchwork.   I. Title.
  TT835.M39963 1998
  746.46--dc21   97-43176

Published by C&T Publishing, Inc.
P.O. Box 1456
Lafayette, California 94549

Printed in Hong Kong
10 9 8 7 6 5 4 3

Preface

A BRIEF HISTORY OF PIECING

From ancient times, people have been joining small pieces of fabric together to get larger ones and recycling scraps from other projects together to make usable pieces of material. The scraps of the different fabrics often made attractive designs in the process. Exploiting this, patchworkers intentionally cut up larger pieces of cloth and stitched them in deliberate patterns to please the eye.

In America, this process eventually resulted in the traditional patchwork blocks, designed usually from a geometric base. As the quiltmaking community pursued this art, quilters' desires to piece more elaborate or creative quilts pushed the craft of sewing bits of cloth together further and further.

I have been fascinated by the piecing process for twenty-five years. My artistic medium is patchwork, assembled on a home sewing machine, and then quilted to sculpt the final surface. In order to produce the images I have in mind, I have pushed myself to try to find my limits in piecing, then work against those limits in developing my pieces. In the process, I have done some hard thinking about the process of pieced design. Particular choices in setting out the piecing design have implications for the visual impact of the quilt, and slight changes from the way most traditional blocks are set up can have significant impact on the final design. Yet, the design of the piecing is but an initial step. It is followed by the much more complicated business of selecting fabric for each piece. Then, upon completion of the pieced top, the design and execution of the quilting stitches hold the layers together and serve to sculpture the surface.

With this book, I will focus on the piecing part of the process, trying to show both the technical piecing techniques that work for me and the design choices and their implications that quiltmakers might consider in laying out original designs of their own.

This book is intended for those who have mastered the basics of sewing quilt blocks and are interested in developing original designs. I will assume that the readers of this book have acquired sewing machine skills and a basic understanding of the piecing process. There are many sources of instruction in basic patchwork, with teachers, classes, shops, and books available worldwide. However, there are few, if any, books that address the potential choices available in the piecing process and their visual implications for design.

Table of Contents

PART 3: DESIGNING

Detail of *Arrowhead,* shown on page 84.

Piecing Straight Seams

The vast majority of traditional quilt blocks are geometric designs, usually symmetrical and usually assembled with straight seams. Originally quilt blocks were pieced by hand, but most quiltmakers nowadays assemble them on the sewing machine.

TEMPLATES VS FOUNDATION PIECING

When I began quiltmaking in 1972, most quilt pieces were cut from templates. For machine piecing, the quiltmaker added ¼" seam allowances to the outline of each piece. Template piecing was a required part of the craft of assembling pieced quilts. Since then, quick-piecing and strip-piecing methods and foundation or paper piecing have taken over in many situations where the ease or quickness of assembly is the primary focus.

After experimenting with the different methods, I have chosen to rely mostly on templates in piecing my quilts. This is for several reasons. First, there are many pieced straight-seam designs which cannot be assembled on a foundation without adapting the design or subdividing the foundation. An example is curved seam designs, which are not appropriate for foundation piecing in almost any case. Second, and almost as important to me, the direction in which the seam allowances are pressed is determined by the order of the paper-piecing process.

Choosing Which Direction to Press Seam Allowances

In order to sculpt the surface of the quilt, I like to be in complete control of the seam allowances. When the quilting is done on the background, close to the seam, the patch under which the seam allowances are pressed can be lifted from the surface of the quilt by the extra padding provided by the seam allowance.

For instance, in *Coffee and Conversation*, pressing the seam of the front rim of each cup away from the lip, and quilting closely above the seam, lifts the front rim forward and pushes the coffee and back rim back. Similarly, the coffee/back rim seam is pressed under the coffee, and the back rim/background seam under the rim. Controlling the direction in which each seam is pressed allows me to sculpture the cups in the low relief of the quilting process. There are even instances where pressing a seam open is a better solution, another technique not possible with foundation piecing.

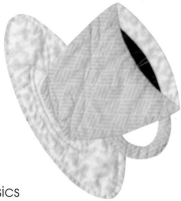

Coffee and Conversation

1995, 55" x 52"

machine pieced, three

hand-appliquéd cups,

machine quilted,

cottons, cotton batting

(artist's collection)

Economy of Time with String Piecing

Multiple blocks can be assembled much more quickly using templates, string piecing pairs of patches for all the blocks at once.

The eight pieced blocks of this eggplant quilt are all made from the same fabric scheme. Since four blocks are the reverse of the original blocks, the fabrics were stacked with four layers face up and four layers face down and ironed firmly together with a steam iron. Using plastic templates that included the ¼" seam allowances on top of the stack, I could cut through all eight layers at once. With all the pieces cut and carefully arranged, I began to assemble eight blocks at once, sewing the first piece to the second piece eight times.

If I had sewn each block completely, before beginning the next, it would have taken three or four times as long to make all eight as it did with the string-piecing process.

Black Beauty
1987, 49.5" x 60"
machine pieced,
hand appliquéd fruits
and flowers, hand
quilted, cottons, silks,
and blends,
polyester batting
(private collection)

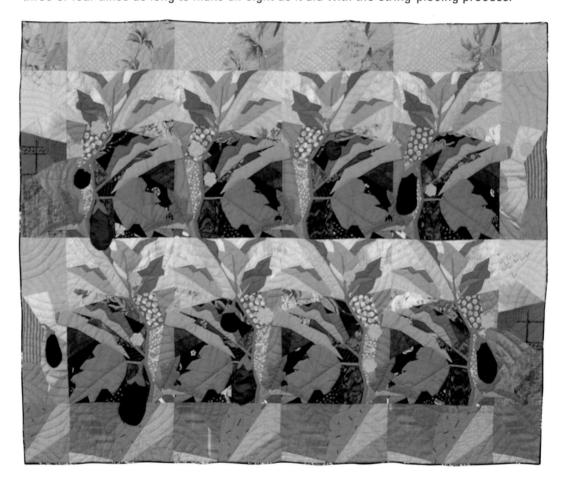

Economy of Fabric with Templates

Template piecing saves a considerable amount of fabric over that required for a foundation-piecing technique. Pieces can be cut economically, with little waste to be trimmed away.

Useful Situations for Foundation Piecing

There are particular instances, however, when foundation piecing is extremely useful. Very small strips or points that need to be sewn in multiples, in which seam direction is not crucial, may be easier to handle this way. Also, foundation piecing can be useful in Log Cabin type constructions and in linear strips.

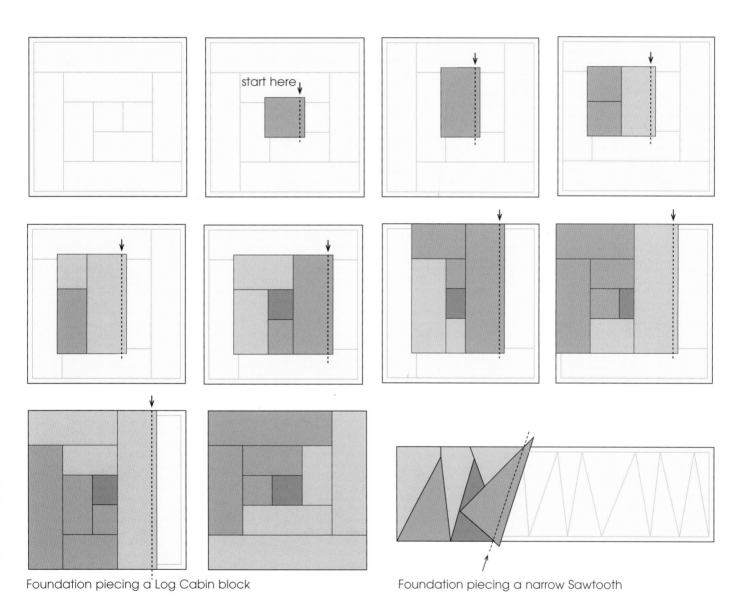

Foundation piecing a Log Cabin block

Foundation piecing a narrow Sawtooth

Traditional Straight-Seam Constructions

Shown here are two basic traditional quilt patches that you may have encountered. Each can be pieced from four patches cut from a single template. Matching the corners, edges, and crossing seams are basic patchwork skills.

SEWING A FOUR-PATCH BLOCK

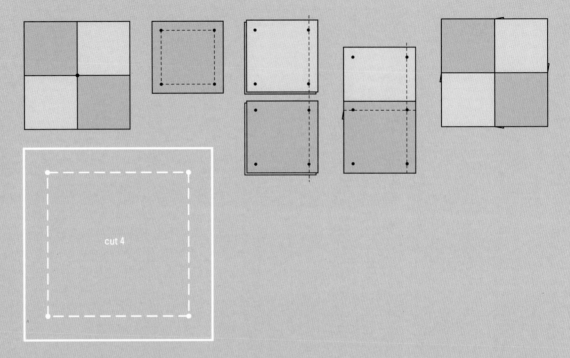

SEWING A BROKEN DISHES BLOCK

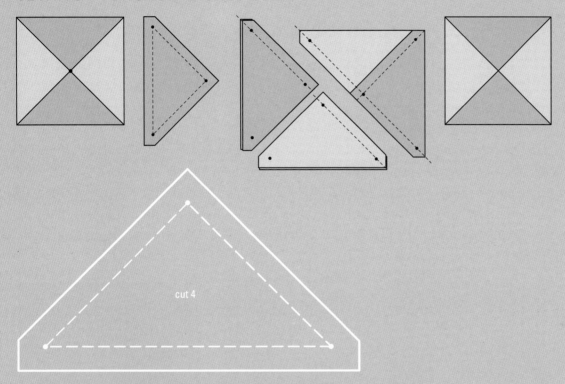

Practice both template piecing and foundation piecing so that you are adept with each. There are several ways to make templates and several backings for foundation piecing. Find a method that works for you and use it.

Piecing Curved Seams

Many quilters have developed individual techniques for handling curves. I assemble them by clipping the seam allowance on the concave piece. The depth and closeness of the clips will vary with the tightness of the radius of the curve. Very gentle curves may require no clipping. Tight radii may require clips every ⅛" extending almost all the way into the seam. In the finished quilt the backing/batting/quilting stitches take the strain from the quilt seam. You will not need the stay stitching used in sewing clothing.

Limits to Curves

A few traditional blocks require curved seams, for instance Mill Wheel, Drunkard's Path, Orange Peel, and Double Wedding Ring. These can be sewn with a template method, but cannot be foundation pieced.

Technically, there are practical limits to the kind of curves that can be sewn with traditional piecing methods. Gentle curves with large radii are easier than tight curves. A radius of ½" is extremely difficult. (Use an appliqué technique, on page 18, for very tight curves or very irregular lines.)

In order to keep the very irregular edge on the foliage of these Monterey pines in *Pas de Deux*, the foliage was done with hand appliqué. The other, smoother curves in the trunks were machine pieced.

Pas de Deux
1989, 67.5" x 46"
machine pieced,
hand appliquéd,
machine quilted,
cottons, textile paint,
cotton batting
(private collection)

Blueprint for an Ancient Implement

1997, 67" x 88"

machine pieced,

machine quilted,

cottons, ink,

cotton batting

(artist's collection)

SEWING A GENTLE CURVE

Pin together the endpoints of the two patches with the concave one on top. You may not have to pin the center points together or to clip the concave edge, depending on the radius of the curve and the flexibility of the fabric.

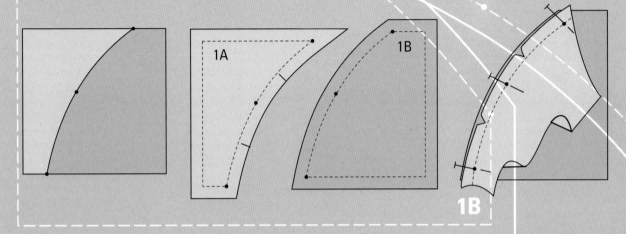

A SLIGHTLY TIGHTER RADIUS CURVE

Clip the concave edge and pin in at least four places for this tighter curve.

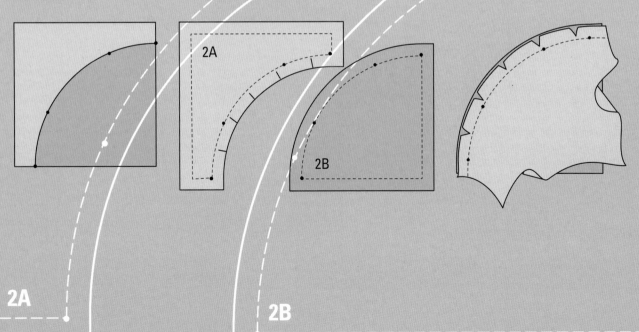

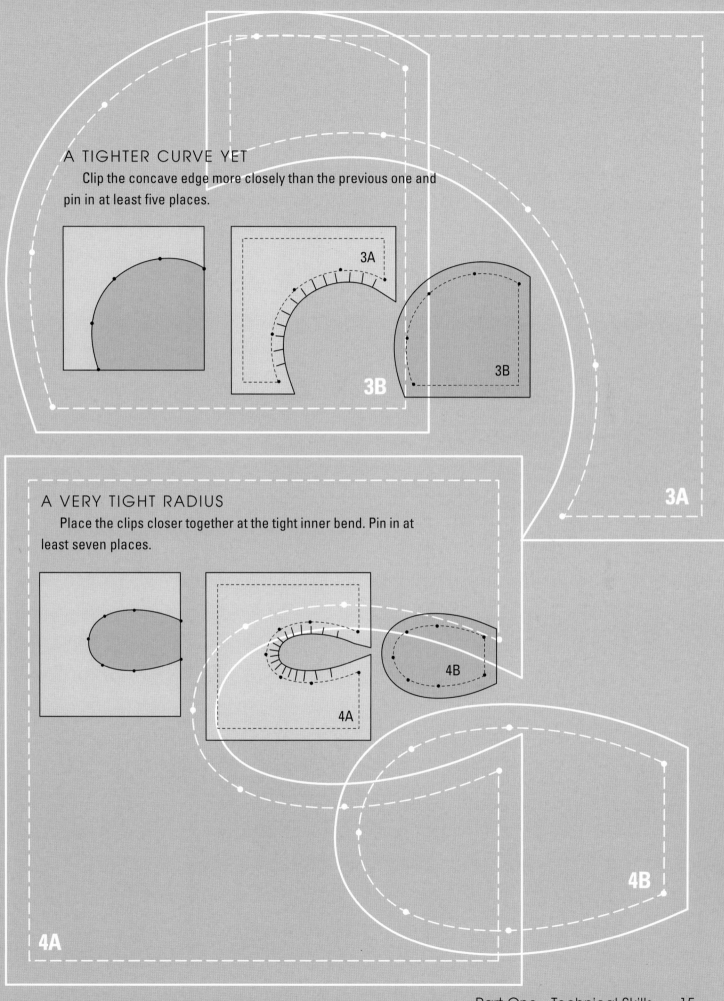

A TIGHTER CURVE YET

Clip the concave edge more closely than the previous one and pin in at least five places.

3A

3B

3B

3A

A VERY TIGHT RADIUS

Place the clips closer together at the tight inner bend. Pin in at least seven places.

4A

4B

4A

4B

SEWING S CURVES

With S curves, part of the seam is concave on each piece. You may find this seam easier to manage if you sew it in two short sections, putting the piece with the concave edge on top while sewing each part of the seam. Placing piece A on top of B, sew from point 1 to point 2. Turn the unit over, then sew from point 3 to point 2.

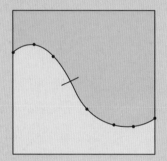

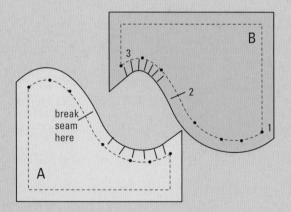

Lotus

a four panel set

1996, each 38.5" x 30"

machine pieced,

machine quilted,

cottons,

cotton batting

(private collection)

Practice several methods with varying radius curves. There are many books and many teachers offering different solutions to machine piecing curved seams. I prefer to pin and clip, clipping more closely, almost all the way to the seamline, for tight curves, and removing the pins as I get to them in the sewing process. Find a method that works for you and use it. In developing your own designs, you may find that you need to modify or adapt your drawings to the degree of curvature you are able to sew.

Handling Very Tight Curves

If very tight curves are a necessary part of the design, consider stitching the straight parts of the seam, stopping before and after the tight section. Then hand piece or appliqué the curved portion.

The shape of the branches in *Moon Gate* seemed to require curved seams. Most of the branches, foliage, and landscape are machine pieced. A few of the tight curves and small branches are appliquéd, as are the figures. The foliage was very dense. Using plaids at angles, piecing with curved seams, and then highlighting with a few reverse hand appliqués worked well.

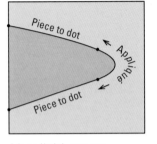

Very tight curves

Moon Gate

1989, 51" x 120"

machine pieced,

hand appliquéd,

hand quilted,

cottons, blends,

polyester batting

(private collection)

One of the fabrics that was very useful is the large navy-and-cream print on the dunes under the trees. Rhoda Cohen donated this to my stash several years before this quilt was made with the comment, "Here, you need this." I couldn't figure out where to use it in a top, and used some as a back. The scale and pattern of this print and the degree of contrast in values make perfect shadows under the pine tree, and complement the other fabrics. The print could have been almost any dark and light color and would have worked as well. The grass fabric in the borders and lower left is an old Marimekko® screen-printed cotton.

Mastering these assembly methods is part of your craft. As you become more adept, you will find you can greatly expand your ability to sew complicated pieces.

Piecing Insets

When piecing a quilt, the quiltmaker can take some liberties, especially for wall quilts that will not get severe handling, that are more questionable than when sewing clothing. When the quilt is finished and the quilting stitching done, the strain on the individual seams is distributed across the whole quilt. Therefore, inset corners such as the ones you may find on a square yoke on a bodice are a possibility for patchwork. Save inset corners for closely woven fabrics, and use a smaller stitch length for the seam, clipping to the corner before you begin to sew.

INSETTING A WIDE ANGLE

Clip the corner of the concave piece almost to the dot at point 2. Put piece A on top of piece B, right sides together, matching points 1 and 2, then carefully pinning them together. Starting at point 1, sew to point 2 and stop. Leaving the needle in the fabric, raise the presser foot, pull point 3 of piece A to match point 3 of piece B. Carefully pin the pieces together. Pivot both pieces on the needle, lower the presser foot, and complete sewing the seam.

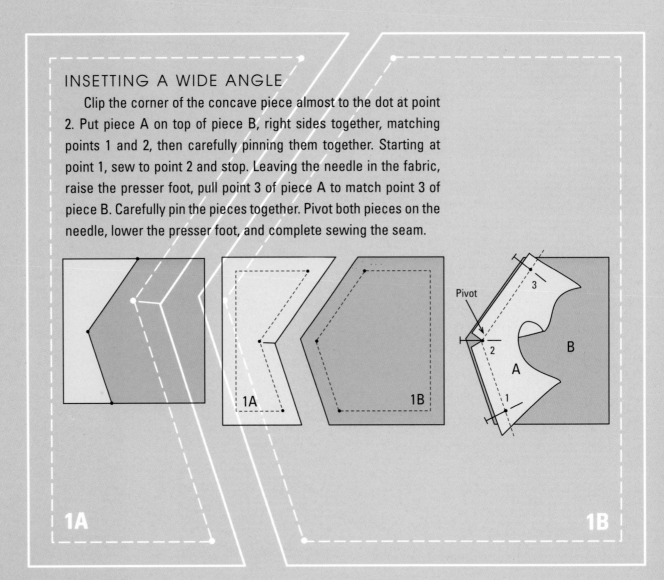

Cyclamen

1985, 48.5" x 65"

machine pieced,

hand appliquéd,

hand and machine

quilted, cottons

and blends,

polyester batting,

netting

(private collection)

The 144° angle at the base of the Penrose darts used in *Cyclamen* (in three sizes) is easily handled with an inset seam.

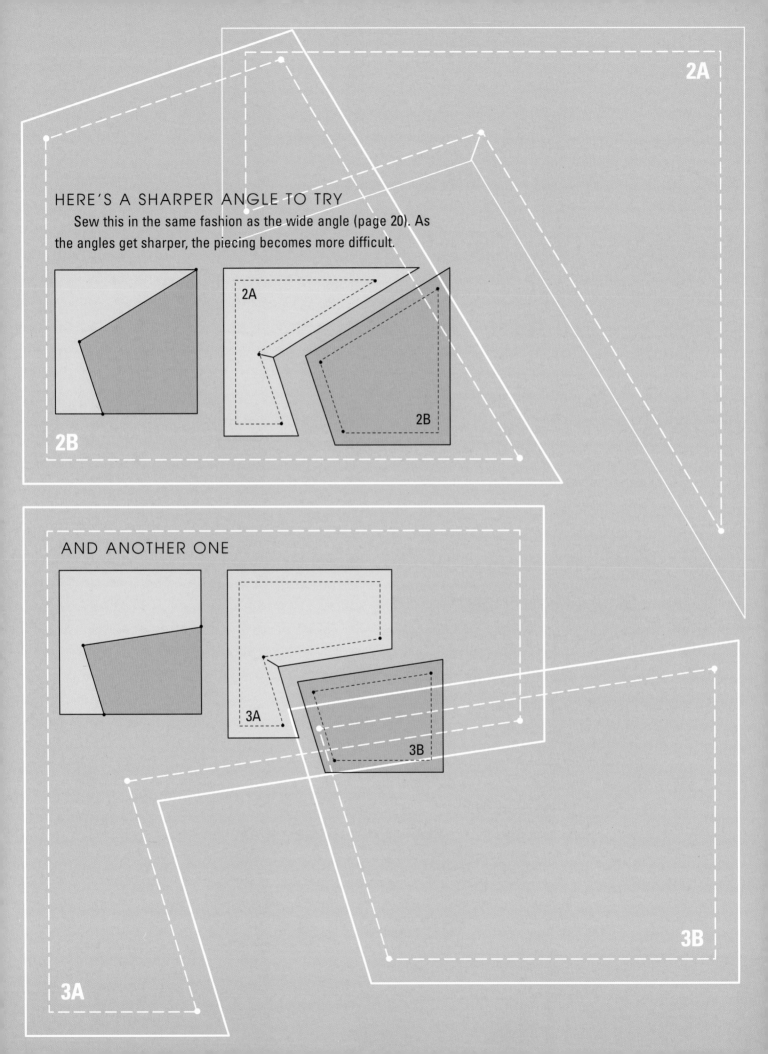

HERE'S A SHARPER ANGLE TO TRY

Sew this in the same fashion as the wide angle (page 20). As the angles get sharper, the piecing becomes more difficult.

2B

2A

2B

AND ANOTHER ONE

3A

3B

2A

3A

3B

AND ANOTHER ONE

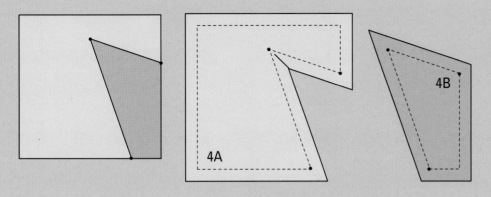

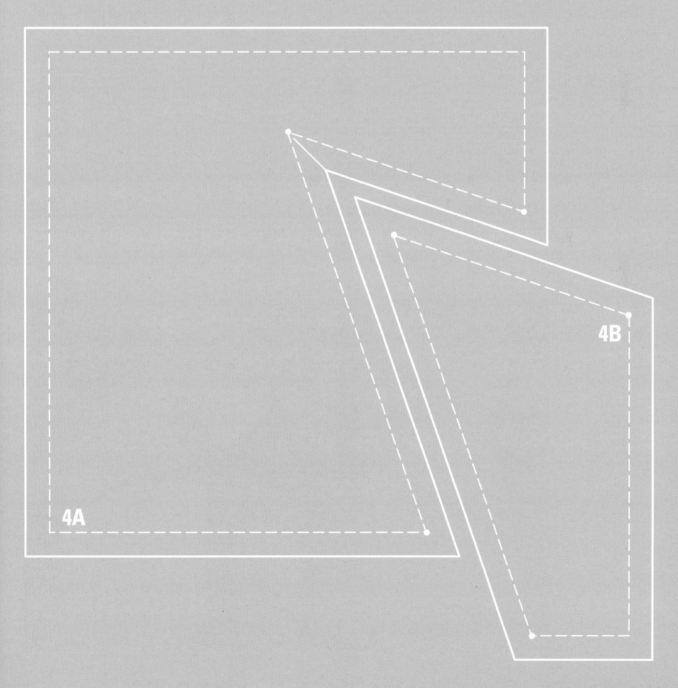

Beside the Sea
1993, 53" x 84.5"
machine pieced,
machine quilted,
cottons, cotton batting
(artist's collection)

All of the foliage of these Monterey cypresses was cut from a single fabric in an experiment in making a landscape from very few fabrics. Inset corners enabled me to sew it without having to cut the foliage into tiny bits, and preserved some of the character of the tie-dyed fabric.

A VERY SHARP ANGLE (LESS THAN 60°)

If you can manage this angle, you are ready for almost anything. It may be easier to abandon the pivot method and sew each side separately, backstitching at the point. You might also consider the use of Fray Check™ or a scrap of lightweight iron-on interfacing to reinforce the point.

A tailoring technique may be useful as well: Stitch the first seam as usual, pivot halfway on the needle at the point, and take one stitch across the tip of the point. Pivot again on the needle and stitch the second seam.

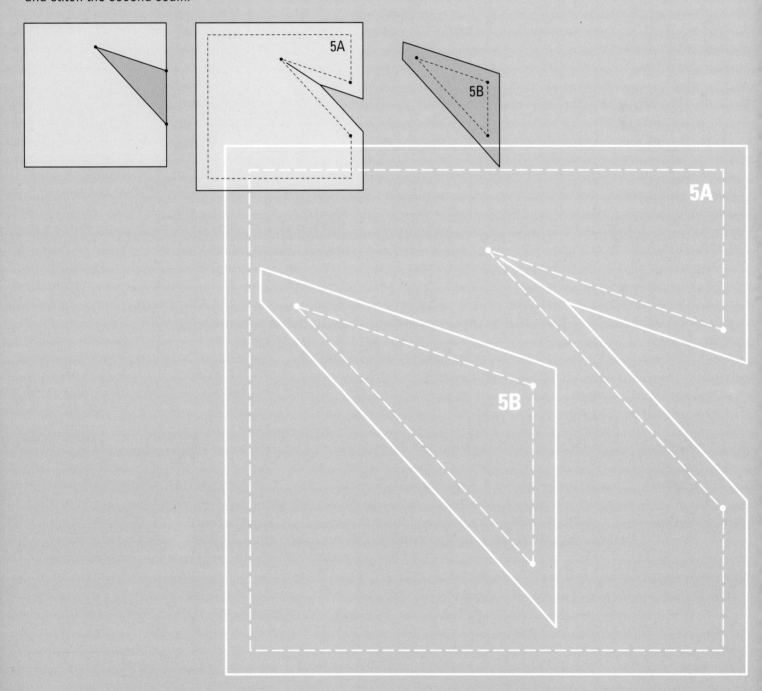

SEWING Z SEAMS

For a Z seam, place piece A on top of B and sew from points 1 to 2 to 3, then stop. Make a couple of small backstitches at 3. Remove the unit from the machine and turn it over. Match and pin point 4. Sew this last piece of seam, with B on the top, backstitching again at point 3.

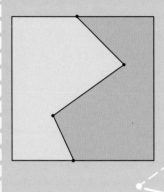

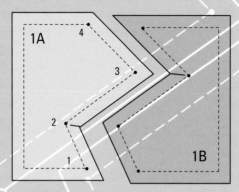

SEWING MULTIPLE ANGLES

For two angles, proceed as above, but clip both inset corners before you begin. Pivot at the second inset corner when you get to it as you did at the first.

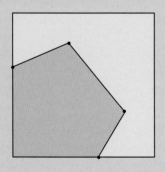

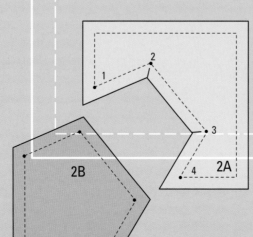

Outgrowth

1996, 66" x 47"

machine pieced,

machine quilted,

cottons, cotton batting

(private collection)

Sewing insets and Z's allowed me to keep the angularity of the branches in *Outgrowth* without fracturing the background pieces into very small bits.

INSET ANGULAR PATCHES

It is possible to use these techniques to inset one piece of fabric into another using a sewing machine. The ease with which you can do this will depend on practice, the shape and size of the pieces, and the weave of the fabric. It is usually quicker for me to piece an inset patch on the machine instead of appliquéing the patch (and pruning away the material behind the patch). Prepare the pieces by leaving a seam allowance inside the seamline for the background, and outside the seamline for the patch. Mark the seamline on the back of both pieces.

Primroses

1985, 44" x 42"

machine pieced, hand quilted, fringed, cottons and blends, polyester batting (private collection)

The primrose flowers were pieced as separate pentagonal blocks, then machine pieced into holes cut in the leaf blocks. There will be a size limit below which this construction becomes difficult. Practice to determine what your limit is for patches of various shapes. For patches smaller than you are comfortable with, appliqué by hand or machine, trimming away excess fabric behind the patch.

INSETTING AN ANGLED PATCH

Carefully clip to the corners of the background piece. With the patch right side up, lay one wrong side edge of the background piece on top, matching and pinning corners 1 and 2. Start sewing in the middle of this seam. Sew to corner 2, pivot, then match and pin corner 3. Continue in this way until you get back to where you began.

As you saw with inset corners, this technique will be more practical if the angles of the patch are greater than 60°. Insetting triangles will be difficult.

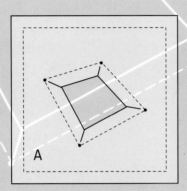

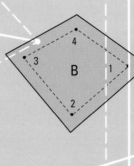

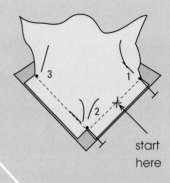

start here

A

B

White Baneberry

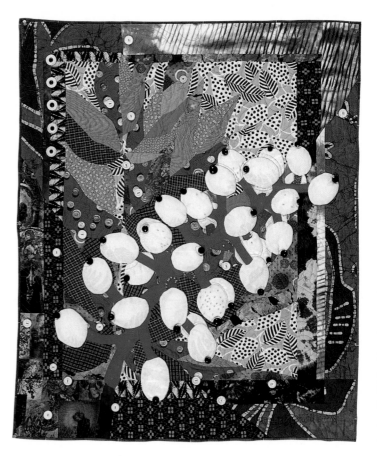

White Baneberry 1
1996, 43" x 35"
machine pieced,
hand appliquéd,
machine quilted,
cottons, buttons,
cotton batting
(private collection)

INSET CIRCULAR SHAPES

This machine piecing technique was employed to piece in the white berries of *White Baneberry 1* and *White Baneberry 2* (page 32). There will be a size limit below which this construction becomes difficult. Practice to determine what your limit is for patches of varying shapes. For patches smaller than you are comfortable with insetting, appliqué by hand or machine, trimming away excess fabric behind the patch.

I find the inset technique useful in many of my designs because it allows me to eliminate some construction seams.

INSETTING A CIRCULAR SHAPE

Now try an inset circular shape. Because this patch is not a perfect circle, it will only fit into the hole one way. Mark the seamline and dots on the back of both pieces. Mark the notch at the starting point.

Clip the edge of the background piece. With the patch right side up on the bottom, match the background and pin the notches first. Now match and pin the rest of the dots, spreading out the clips. Stitch the seam, starting at the notch, and easing the clips open to fit as you proceed.

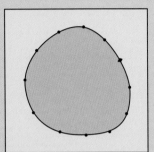
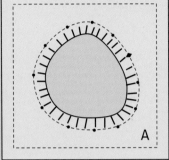
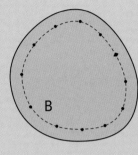
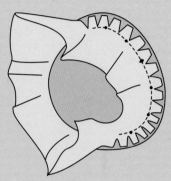

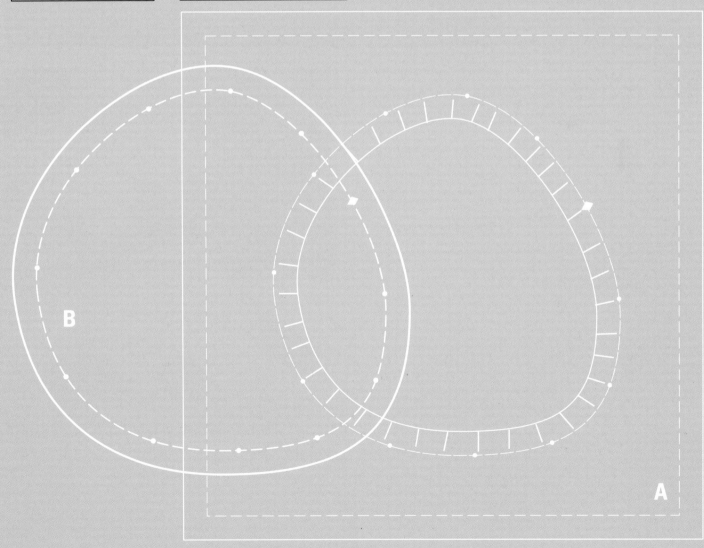

White Baneberry 2
1996, 53" x 77.5"
machine pieced, hand
appliquéd, machine
quilted, cottons, linen,
blends, cotton batting
(artist's collection)

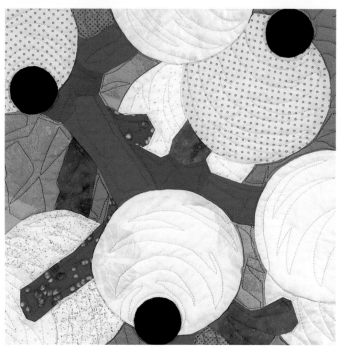

The white berries in the two baneberry quilts are pieced in by machine as part of my normal piecing process. They are between four and six inches across. The black dots in *White Baneberry 2* are hand appliquéd. They are about two inches in diameter.

Piecing Puzzles

DEFINING PUZZLES

You may have found this type of piecing in some traditional quilt blocks. It happens when a piece is locked into several others, making simple assembly impossible.

Painted Daisies

1992, 69" x 69"

machine pieced,

hand quilted by Carol

Marrochello, cottons,

cotton batting

(private collection)

CONSTRUCTION OF PUZZLE SEAMS

To sew this kind of construction, you will need to sew a partial seam, complete several other seams, and finally finish the partial seam to complete the block.

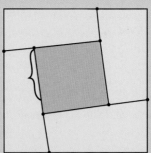

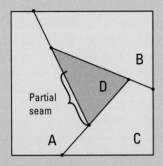

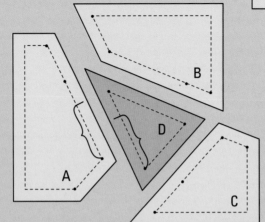

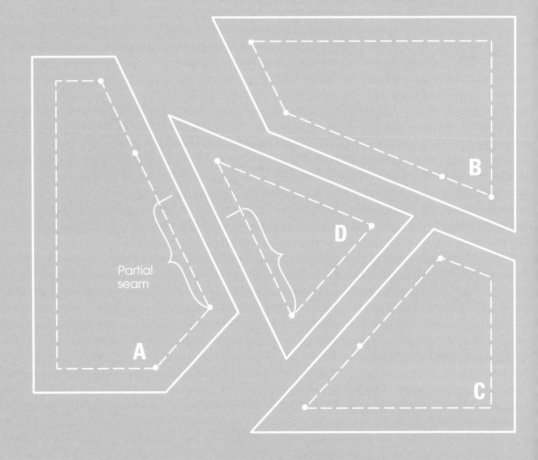

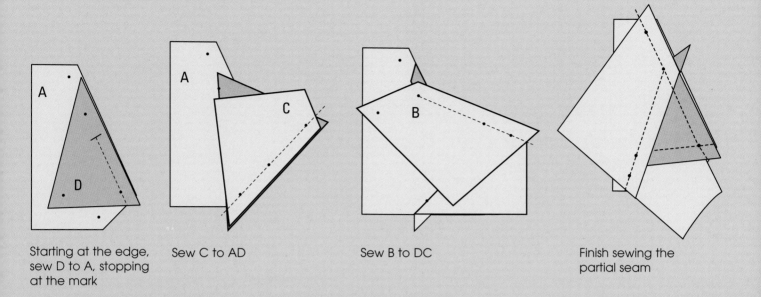

Starting at the edge, sew D to A, stopping at the mark

Sew C to AD

Sew B to DC

Finish sewing the partial seam

CHANGING THE DESIGN TO ELIMINATE PUZZLES

You may prefer to change the piecing of the design to another pattern of seams.

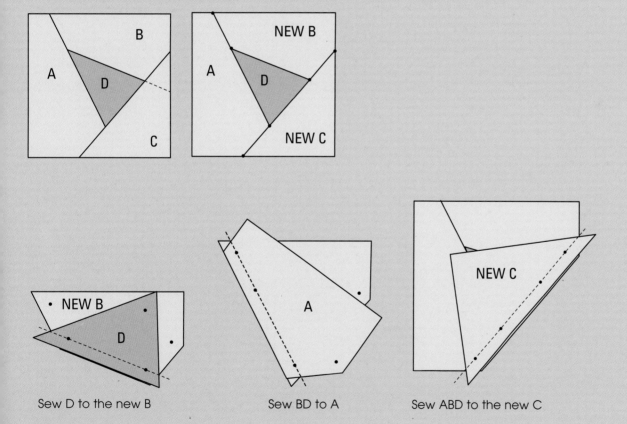

Sew D to the new B

Sew BD to A

Sew ABD to the new C

Or for another example of puzzle elimination, see the piecing diagrams of the Grizzly Bear section (pages 112-117).

Piecing Y's and y's

Joining three pieces of fabric together in traditional blocks can make two types of Y seam.

DEFINING y SEAMS

In the first instance, piece B is sewn to piece A with a straight seam edge to edge. Then the AB piece is joined to piece C, again with a straight seam edge to edge. This is a simple construction to make. Let's call it the "y" seam (lowercase y).

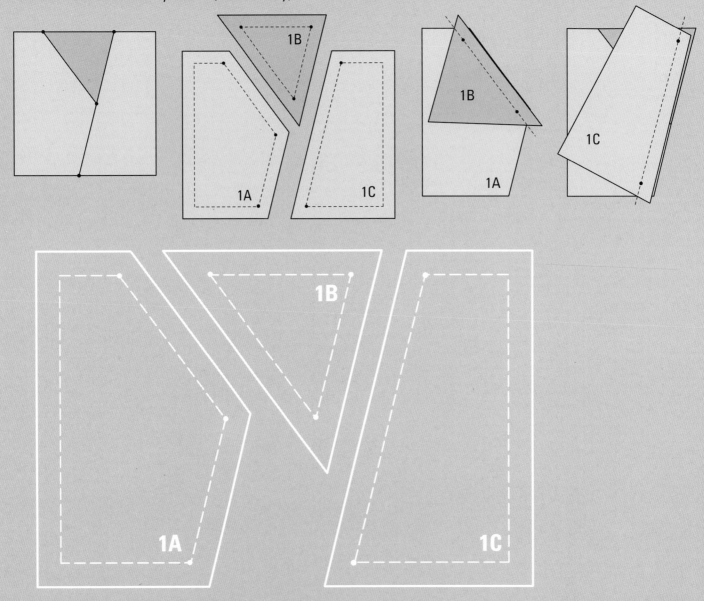

DEFINING Y SEAMS

Or you may begin with a diagram like this one, which we'll call a "Y" seam (uppercase Y).

Here piece B is sewn to piece A with a small backstitch at the inner corner. Then piece C is joined to piece A, again with a small backstitch at the inner corner. Finally, piece B is sewn to piece C with a small backstitch at the inner corner.

The Y seam is simple if pieced by hand. With machine piecing this is a much more awkward construction than the first y seam. As you work on your design, consider which type to use. A slight change in the design may enable you to change from Y's to y's, making the piecing much simpler.

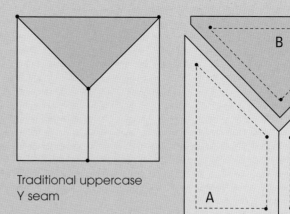

Traditional uppercase Y seam

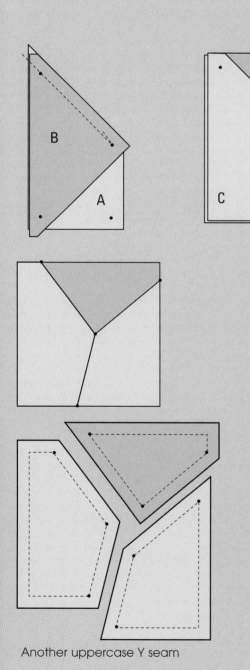

Another uppercase Y seam

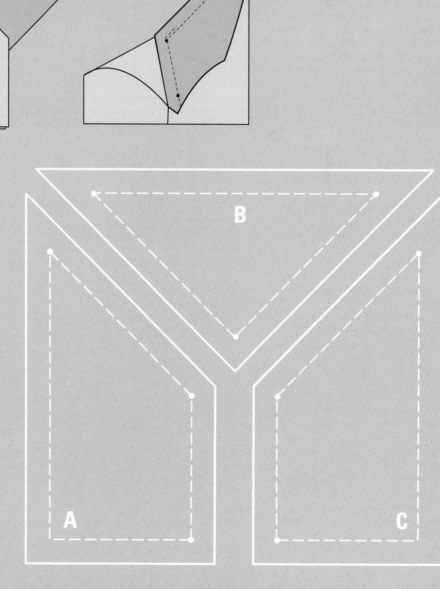

Many tessellations require Y seams, as in this detail from *Sunflowers* (on page 45), a combination of regular hexagons, squares, and equilateral triangles.

ADAPTING Y'S TO y's FOR MACHINE PIECING

You may prefer Y's to express a particular visual concept. Or you may want to change one of the seams of the Y to make a y to simplify the sewing.

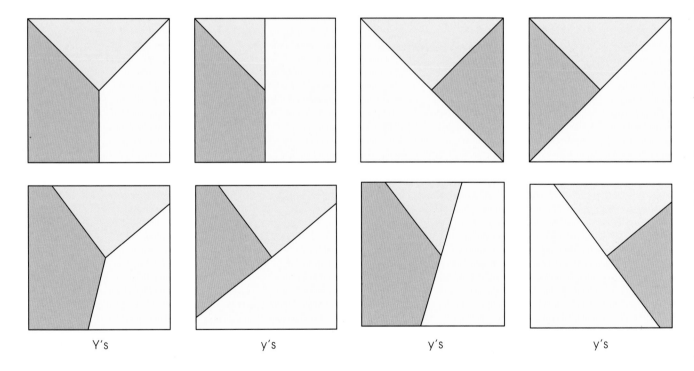

Y's   y's   Y's   y's

CHANGING Y SEAMS TO X SEAMS

Extending one Y seam to a block edge makes the Y into an X to simplify machine piecing. If piece A and piece D are made of the same fabric, the visual appearance will not be much different from the Y seam construction.

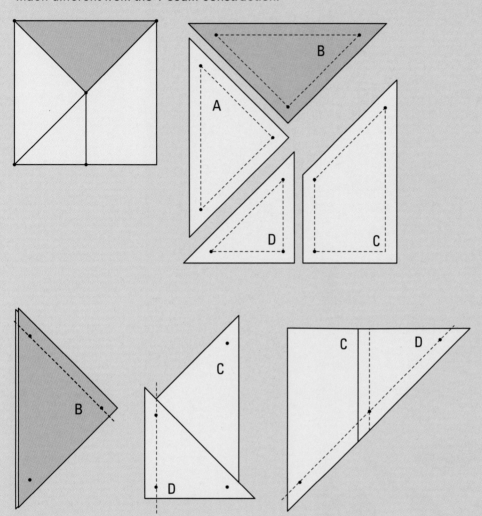

Sew B to A   Sew D to C   Sew AB to CD

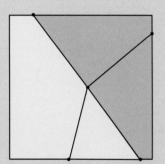

Another Y seam changed
to an X seam

Lilies

1984, 46" x 41"

machine pieced,
hand quilted, hand
appliquéd over
borders, cottons and
blends, polyester
batting
(private collection)

There are a number of Y seams and y seams in the Lilies block. I could have changed the Y's within the block to y's by adding or extending some seams. In this case, I decided I'd rather keep each petal a single piece of fabric and sew Y's than subdivide the petals into more pieces.

In working out this straight-seam pieced block (one half of an orchid flower) from a careful drawing of an orchid blossom, I have employed y seams wherever possible in dividing the background. Notice that they are shifted away from the upper corners.

I didn't want to subdivide the petals any more than necessary, so there are several inset corners and Y seams within the flower. Hand appliqué was used to add the lower bright orange curled lip to the center parts.

Moth Orchids
1992, 74" x 106"
machine pieced, hand
appliquéd, machine
quilted, cottons,
cotton batting
(artist's collection)

Diagonals

TRADITIONAL DIAGONAL INTERSECTIONS

Most traditional blocks, when they are divided on the diagonal, require the sewing of two right triangles together precisely to the corner (Broken Dishes blocks). When joining four of these blocks together, eight seams will come to a single point. This intersection can become bulky and awkward.

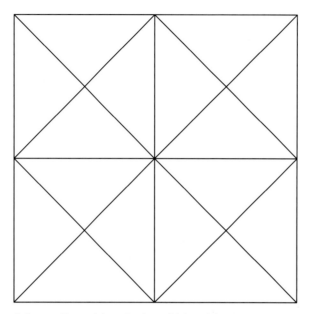

Intersection of four Broken Dishes blocks

MOVING DIAGONALS

As you create your original designs for piecing, consider trying a number of slight changes over most traditional piecing methods.

Consider twisting the right angle lines that meet in the center of the Broken Dishes block away slightly from the corners of the block. As long as the center of the X is in the center of the square block, the new block—a Pinwheel—can still be cut with one template. Joining four blocks together then becomes simpler and cleaner.

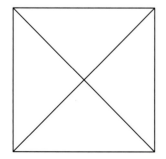 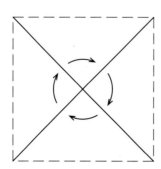 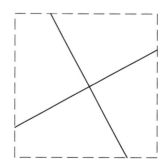 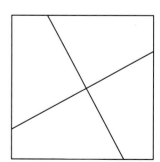

Twisting the diagonal seams away from the corners

PINWHEEL BLOCKS

The overall visual effect of the pattern of Broken Dishes is different from the Pinwheel pattern. Broken Dishes is quite traditional and rather static; Pinwheel is more unusual, has visual motion, and implies a spin. Decide which effect is appropriate for your particular instance.

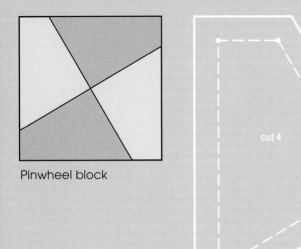

Pinwheel block

cut 4

Intersection of four Pinwheel blocks

EQUILATERAL TRIANGLE AND HEXAGONAL BLOCKS

With Equilateral Triangle blocks or Hexagonal blocks, moving the diagonals from the corners makes a difference in the overall pattern and a difference in the process of sewing groups of blocks together.

Equilateral triangle block variations

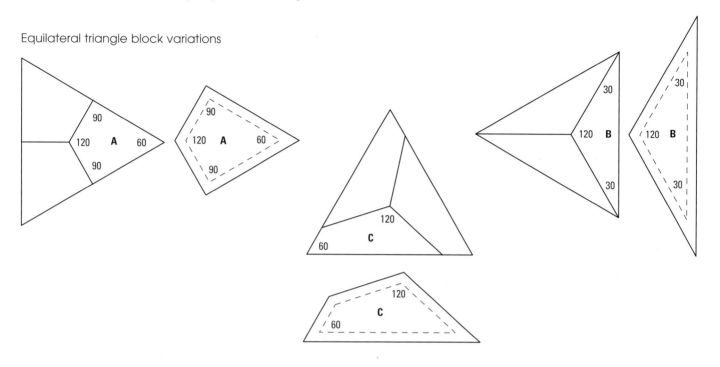

Hexagonal block variations

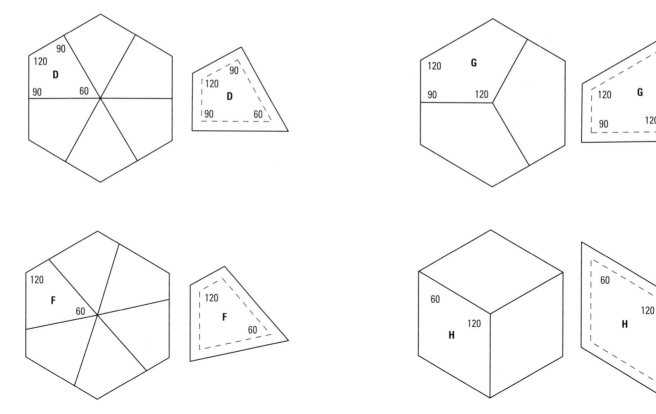

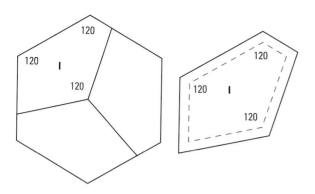
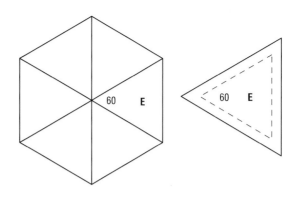

Within the *Sunflowers* below, there is some internal piecing in the square and equilateral triangle units, which allows for piecing of the sunflower petals.

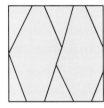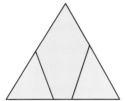

Piecing units for sunflower petals   Faced additional petal flaps

Because these units are joined at the corners with two or three other units, I have intentionally kept the seams away from the corners of the square and triangle so that the intersections are as clean as possible.

Sunflowers
1990, 51" x 66.5"
machine pieced,
machine quilted,
inserted additional
petal flaps, cottons,
polyester batting
(artist's collection)

Linear Elements

The fabric patches used in pieced quilts are just that: pieces of cloth of a particular size. They have a length and a width. Occasionally a patchwork design calls for a very narrow line, for example, the stem of a plant, the trunk of a tree, a clothesline, or a stay on a sailboat.

Of course, linear elements can be added to the surface after the patchwork is completed, with embroidery or appliqué, or a line of quilting, paint, or ink. It is interesting to consider how we might incorporate linear elements into the piecing.

At the Crocker Grove
1990, 47" x 36"
machine pieced,
hand appliquéd,
hand quilted, cottons,
silks, blends,
polyester batting
(private collection)

The tree trunks of *At the Crocker Grove* are machine pieced, with the seam allowances pressed under the trunks to round them out. The small branches on the large cypress are hand appliquéd in order to maintain their intricate curves.

CREATING NARROW TEMPLATES

Narrow pieces can be included as templates and sewn into the quilt using a ¼" seam allowance.

Sewing a strip wider than a half inch (finished).

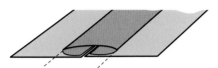

When sewing a half inch (finished) strip, the seam allowances, if pressed toward the center, just touch along the center line. The strip will be padded a little by the extra layers and stand out slightly from the surface of the patchwork. If the seam allowances are pressed away from the center, the strip will appear slightly depressed and the area around it slightly raised.

As the strip decreases from a half inch (finished) to a quarter inch (finished), the seam allowances will begin to overlap if pressed toward the center, which increases the padding under the strip and raises it up further.

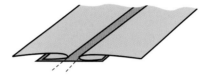

If pressed away from the center, the strip will begin to seem more like a crack, especially if quilted down the center line.

First seam

Second seam

If you try to sew a piece narrower than a quarter inch, and keep both seam allowances free, you will find it technically difficult. When I must have a very narrow piece, I press the first seam toward the center and sew the second seam as usual, sewing right through the seam allowances of the first seam. Then the seams can be trimmed as necessary and pressed in either direction.

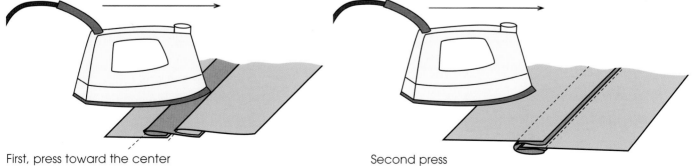

First, press toward the center

Second press

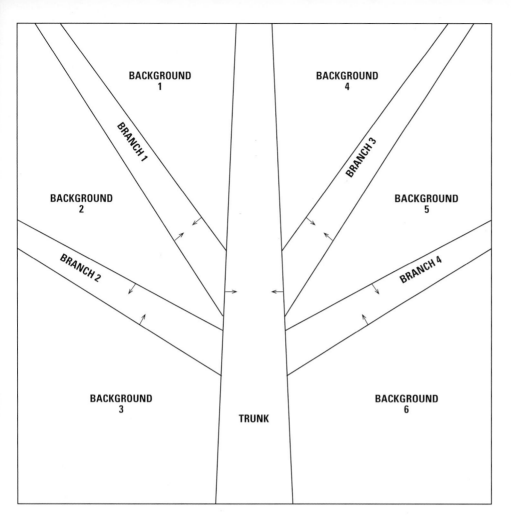

A SMALL TREE MADE WITH NARROW TEMPLATES

I can make this 5" tree block using the narrow template technique (page 47). Use the template to cut the fabric pieces, adding the ¼" seam allowances to each piece. Sew the branches to the background fabric pieces. Press in the direction of the arrows. Add the trunk.

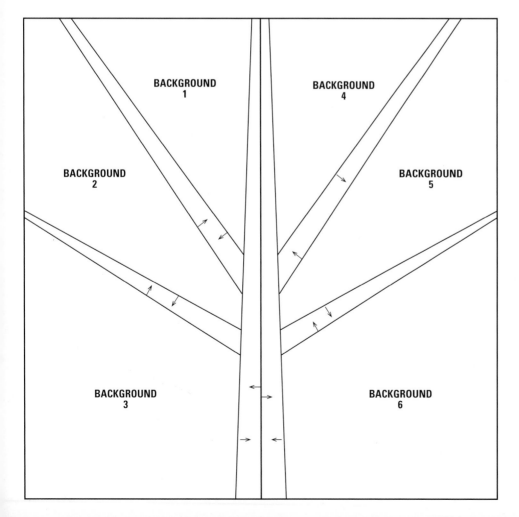

SEW-AND-FLIP TECHNIQUE

I can also make linear elements by a sew-and-flip technique, rather than using a separate template.

To make the little tree block use the background templates from the "invisible" tree on page 52 to cut the background fabric pieces.

Cut strips of fabric for the branches and the tree trunk. If I want, I can vary the exact placement of the sew-and-flip piece from tree to tree, making some branches wider and some narrower.

I can trim the strip after it has been sewn and pressed toward the center to match the edge of the background piece. If desired, I can then trim away some of the background piece under the strip.

MAKING THE LITTLE TREE WITH A SEW-AND-FLIP TECHNIQUE

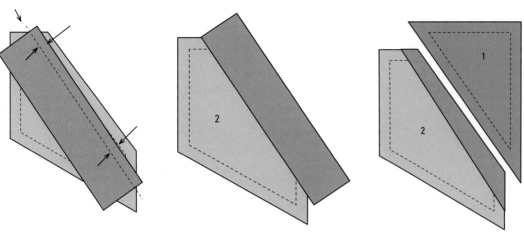

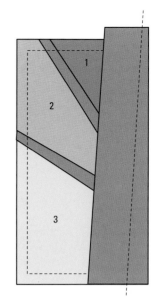

Stitch strips for branches to background pieces 2 and 3. Then press strips along stitched seams, and trim.

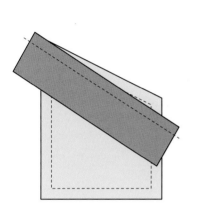

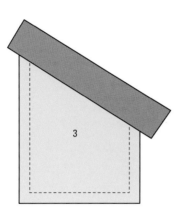

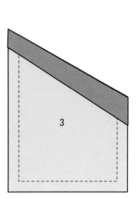

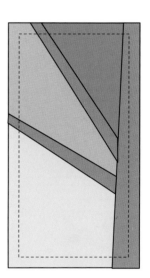

Join background pieces 1,2,3, stitching through all seam allowances.

Press seams under the branches. Add the strip for the trunk in the same manner. Repeat for the other half of the tree, and join the two halves together.

PIPING

Or, I can make the linear element as a folded piece of fabric inserted in the seam before sewing. This is very similar to inserting piping in a seam. If the seam is straight, use a straight grain for the strip. If the seam is curved, use a bias strip.

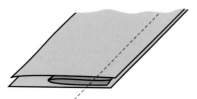

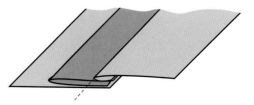

Making a linear element with a folded strip

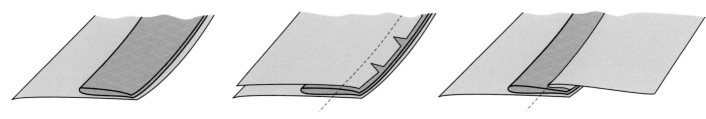

Sewing and pressing a folded bias strip in a curved seam

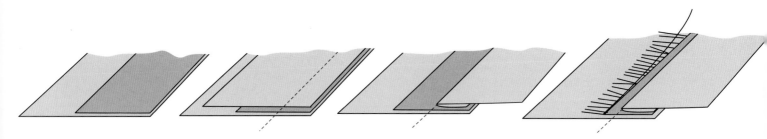

Using a strip with a raw edge on the surface of the quilt. Fringe the strip, if desired.

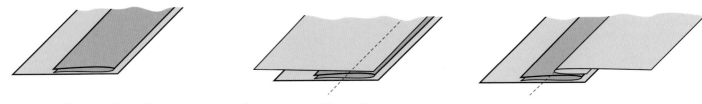

Using a folded strip with raw edges on the surface of the quilt

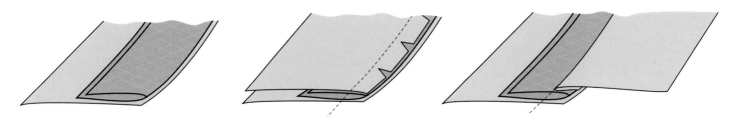

Sewing and pressing the raw edge of a folded strip to a curved seam

The loose edge can be left free, appliquéd by hand or machine, or stitched down with a straight stitch.

"INVISIBLE" TREES

For my earlier quilts, when I was working with plant material in piecing designs, I often pieced in ¼"-wide stems. As I spent more time with the piecing process, I discovered I could leave out the stem itself if I put a major seam where the stem would be. The linearity of the seam would read as a stem, and no one would notice the physical stem was missing, creating an "invisible" tree. Leaving the stem out eliminated a fussy detail, and usually made the visual impact of the piece stronger. This has been an interesting concept to pursue.

Hooker's Primrose and Bamboo

1991, 51" x 31"

machine pieced,

hand appliquéd, hand

quilted, cottons,

polyester batting

(private collection)

Hooker's Primrose and Bamboo was designed to accommodate both the primrose and the bamboo. I chose to place the primrose in the foreground, piecing in the leaves and buds and letting the stem be drawn by a major seam. The seams for the leaves fracture the bamboo and serve to keep the primary focus on the primrose.

Piecing the flowers at this scale, in addition to the other elements, would have meant too many seams and would have sacrificed some of the freedom and delicacy of their curves. Hand appliqué of the flower petals was a good solution.

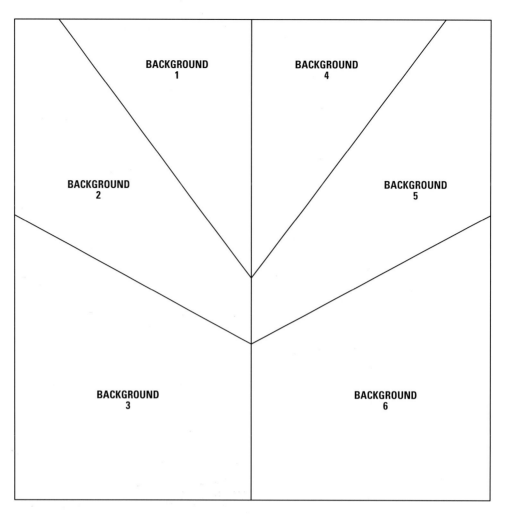

Making an "invisible" tree by letting the stems be drawn by a major seam

On many of my larger pieced tree quilts, I have pieced in the major branches but let simple seamlines represent the twigs at the ends. The seamline twigs will be enhanced if the pieces on either side of the seam are very different fabrics.

White Oak
1990, 36" x 71"
machine pieced,
machine quilted,
cottons, silks,
polyester batting
(private collection)

Or, to make a more subtle twig, use the same plaid, stripe, or large-scale print on both sides of the seam, letting the break in the woven or printed pattern show the seamline.

In the landscape of *Northern Forest*, I have used the "invisible" elements to suggest additional tree trunks in the background and for the horizontal branches growing from the main trunks, rather than using piecing or appliquéing to create this effect as in earlier quilts. I like the way this works.

Northern Forest
1996, 64" x 87"
machine pieced,
machine quilted,
cottons, cotton batting
(private collection)

Regeneration

1996, 61" x 82"

machine pieced,

machine quilted,

cottons, cotton batting

(private collection)

Shifting the Focus

Almost all traditional piecing calls for the precise matching of intersecting seams, as we can see in the Four Patches, Broken Dishes, and even the Pinwheel blocks. Let's look at those seams more closely.

Comparing Four Patch, Broken Dishes, and Pinwheel Blocks

Four Patch, Broken Dishes, and Pinwheel blocks will each make a different visual impact on your design. You have seen Four Patch and Broken Dishes blocks many times before. They focus on the center of the block and the corners. Pieced from a single template, the designs can vary depending on the fabrics used in each of the four sections. As designs, they are very stable, in almost every colorway.

Pinwheel blocks are not as common. As with Four Patch and Broken Dishes blocks, Pinwheels focus on the center and are cut from a single template. They can be varied also by the choice of fabric in the four sections. But as designs, they appear to spin, introducing the element of motion.

INTERSECTING SEAMS

Experienced quiltmakers will have dealt with a traditional Four Patch block many times. The only tricky part of the sewing process is to make the horizontal seams match exactly when sewing together the two halves of the block. But consider what happens to the visual effect of the block if you deliberately make these seams slightly offset.

Looking at the pair of blocks carefully, what is the visual difference between the matching and the off-set or slipped versions? I think the seam that is continuous assumes more importance, becomes stronger, and the interrupted seam becomes secondary or weaker.

With the traditional Four Patch, each seam is of equal importance and the point at their intersection at the center of the block becomes the focus. The slipped versions require more templates, but are easier to sew. The slipped versions are simpler to sew because the central seams do not match precisely. They also offer the chance to place more emphasis on one seam direction over another.

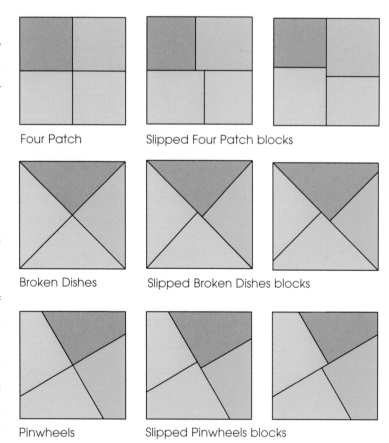

Four Patch   Slipped Four Patch blocks

Broken Dishes   Slipped Broken Dishes blocks

Pinwheels   Slipped Pinwheels blocks

Now, consider Broken Dishes and a Slipped Broken Dishes block, and the Pinwheels and Slipped Pinwheels. Again, more templates are required. The focus shifts from the center, with an equal weight on each element. Within these blocks one seam becomes more prominent than the other.

DEPTH OF FIELD

I think of slipping as a chance to play with depth of field in my piecing, almost in the way I could with a camera. I've chosen to focus on the continuous seam. The interrupted seam is suppressed and slightly out of focus because of the break.

Rainy Day Dances
1995, 37.5" x 35.5"
machine pieced,
machine quilted,
cottons, cotton batting
(private collection)

In *Rainy Day Dances*, the diagonal seams, representing a summer rain, break up the stone wall and the edge of the lawn above the dancers.

MORE VARIATIONS OF SLIPPED BLOCKS

I have kept the blocks (on page 55) almost symmetrical by keeping the intersections close to the block's center. I could move the intersections away from the center as well as slipping the seams.

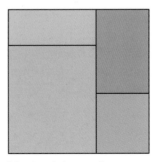 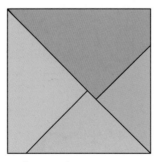 

Moving intersections away from the center

 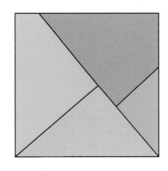 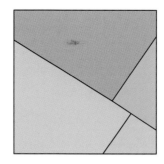

Most of these versions require four templates. The visual results can be very different than the centered versions, yet the sewing is no more difficult. With my piecing, I would rather have more variety. Playing with depth of field fascinates me, cutting the extra templates seems like a minor price to pay for the additional variety of designs that can result.

With the above examples, I am aware that I have just been looking at the skeleton of the block, not the block constructed of fabric. Choice of fabrics, hues, values, chroma, and printed textures in each of the pieces of the design will make these blocks work in different ways. But the slipped intersections will still be a major influence on the finished blocks.

Chameleon Spiral
1996, 41" x 44"
machine pieced,
machine quilted,
cottons, cotton batting
(private collection)

The darker chameleon at the lower left appears to dissolve into the quilt.

Shifting the Focus in a Landscape

Moving the concept of slipped seams and depth of field into more complicated piecing has very interesting results.

A SIMPLE LANDSCAPE TO PIECE

Here's a little fabric scene to make. Six tree trunks of varying sizes form a screen between the viewer and a lake and distant mountain. You will notice with this landscape that I could remove the trees, and the horizontals forming the remaining landscape would make continuous lines.

The pieces of the simple landscape could be cut and pieced in vertical columns. Piecing in columns allows for some variation in fabrics within a single landscape element, that is the "lake" fabric could vary from column to column.

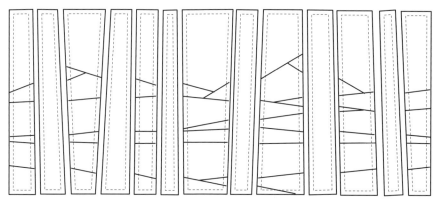

Piecing in columns

Or the entire landscape is pieced first to arrive at the image to the left (below). Then, the landscape is cut along the indicated lines, the six tree trunks cut, and the whole pieced back together. Note that where the trees are narrow, less than 1/2" wide, there will not be a full 1/4" seam allowance on the landscape pieces; and where the tree is wider than 1/2", there will be an extra wide seam allowance that can be trimmed to 1/4". With this method, all of the pieces of the "lake" fabric will be from the same fabric.

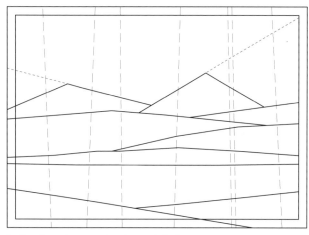

Entire landscape is pieced first

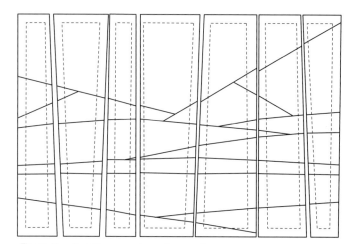

Then the landscape is cut apart

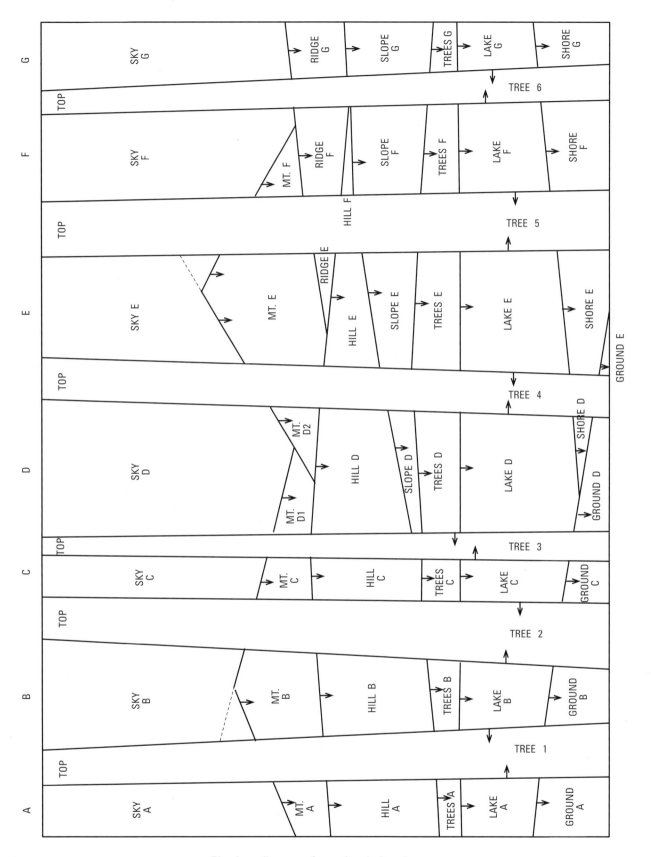

Piecing diagram for a simple landscape

PIECING A SLIPPED LANDSCAPE

Let's begin with a slightly different drawing of my landscape. This time, you will notice that the landscape elements do not form continuous horizontal lines behind the trees. They jog up and down and tip a bit. This version is pieced in columns. Slightly different fabrics can be used for the same element in the different columns, if desired.

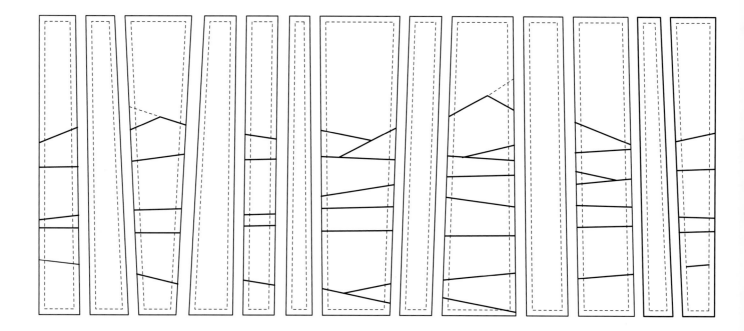

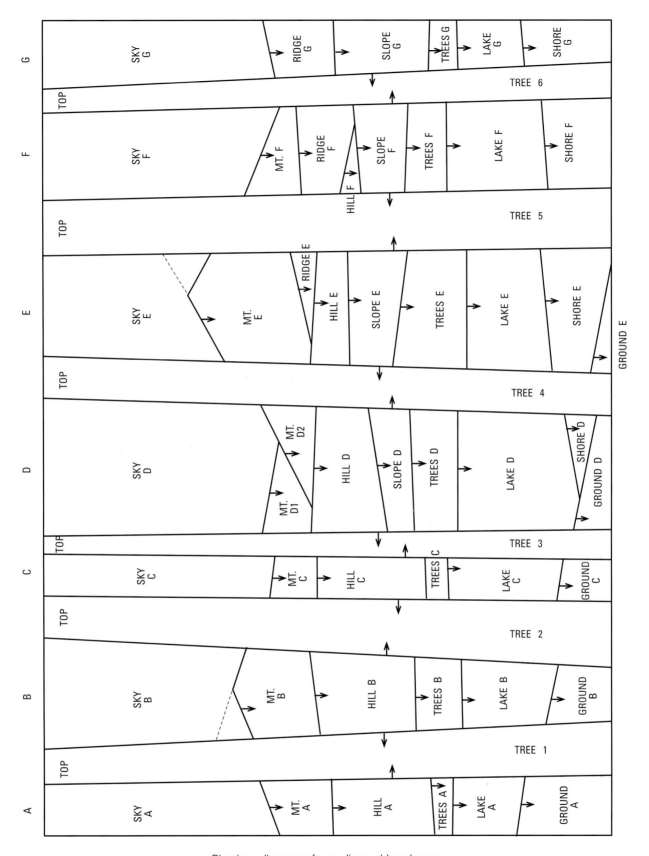

Piecing diagram for a slipped landscape

Simple landscape

COMPARING THE FOCUS

Place the two landscapes side-by-side and study them carefully, looking from one to the other. I think you will agree that in the first landscape you will look through the screen of trees and focus on the distant lake and mountains.

Slipped landscape

In the second landscape, you will find yourself focusing on the trees.

Teaching Guide

You can organize a set of exercises to master the technical elements of Part 1 by using the templates shown throughout the first part of the book. This can be done by an individual, or with a group, or with a teacher as part of a class on piecing. Learning what you are able (and willing) to sew will help determine how to make your designs. The material in this book is not aimed for a quilt-in-a-day audience, but rather for quiltmakers who have mastered basic skills and are ready to begin designing on their own.

ABOUT WORKSHOPS

When teaching a class, I routinely have students of all different levels of experience with a minimum requirement of being able to handle traditional pieced blocks. Some have design backgrounds; others have none. I enjoy the range of experience and find that all of the students and I learn from each other.

Yet, it is crucial to find a way for students to get started designing, at a level that excites, but doesn't overwhelm. Even if that way is straight seams, pieced blocks, or tracing from a photograph, it is a beginning. Mastering this process takes time and practice. The teacher must be ready to encourage and help with students' difficulties, but not set up critical obstacles or rigid rules that could stifle creativity. I prefer to focus on the positive parts of each design, rather than indulging in serious criticism. The students will pick up the negatives quickly enough in what is unsaid.

I'm delighted when each student in a workshop takes off in a different direction. It is tremendously exciting to everyone, but clearly complicates the teacher's role as helper. Each learns at least as much in a multi-day workshop from the other projects being attempted as they do from their own.

Remember that each student has their own learning style and pace, with some more than others finding it easier to function in the confusion of a large workshop. Try to see this as a cooperation in learning rather than a competition in production.

GETTING STARTED

The class can begin with a discussion of piecing and the exercises included in Part 1. In addition to focusing the students on our medium, this helps them determine what kind of sewing they want to attempt.

I then proceed to an easy technical discussion, such as the design of the leaf block. Have the students select a simple object and try to translate that object into a piecing design. Encourage the students to make several different versions of their design with each becoming progressively simpler, and encourage them to use a variety of techniques.

After looking at all of the versions together, suggest that they choose which one with which they would prefer to begin. Talk about why that choice was made and what other possibilities exist. The discussion can be between the teacher and each student, or as a group. Be careful to let each student make his or her own decision, and not be over-whelmed by another decisive or determined individual in the class.

I don't see my role as teacher to be an arbiter of taste. That's the student's department. But I will try to make suggestions about color, composition, and other visual aspects of the design the student chooses.

I remember one student who had made a sketch of a large pieced tree and had included a cartoonish bunny at its base. She was sure she wanted to include the bunny. When she finished working on her tree, drawing to the point where she was ready to sew, she stood back to admire it—and decided the bunny was completely unnecessary.

I also remember another week-long class with a student I'd first met the year before. She was a delightful person who was just beginning her designing career. She'd chosen to work on a quilt of her grandchildren at the beach, and had chosen fabrics for a very brilliant sunset behind them. The colors were brighter than I would have chosen myself, but seemed to be something she really liked. I helped a bit with the design and construction of her quilt and she managed to finish the top by the end of class. In the final wrap-up, as the class as a whole reviewed everyone's projects, she said, as she proudly pinned up her beach scene, "I wonder if I'll still like that bright sunset next week after my cataract operation."

I'm happy to report that she did.

PART TWO DESIGNING ORIGINAL PIECING

A Simple Leaf

PLANNING PIECING FROM A FREEHAND SKETCH

When I set about to make a pieced quilt based on an image from nature, I first prepare a careful line drawing of the image from sketches of the view, or views, I want to use. The careful sketch serves several purposes, but primarily it forces me to spend considerable time carefully investigating the natural image in all its complexities. There will necessarily be an abstraction of the image when translating it into a quilting medium. The more I observe the image, the more easily I am able to distill the essence that can be captured in piecework.

From rough sketches, I work up a careful, detailed line drawing, working at the size I anticipate sewing. I recognize that learning to draw takes a lifetime of practice: The more drawing I do, the better I get. This is a skill that requires work and time. It is preferable to work from the real natural object so you can turn it around, examine it closely, and draw it from different angles. Or, if necessary, make drawings from a photograph (or photographs).

On an even simpler level, prepare a line tracing of a photograph and enlarge it on a copier, or with an opaque projector, to the size of the finished quilt. This process is described in detail in the section on Piecing Complicated Quilts (on page 86).

I prefer not to work from a painting or drawing by another artist, as that imposes someone else's vision between the subject and me; also, using another artist's work introduces several legal concerns over copyright. Try to respond to nature in a very personal way. Notice the ways other artists translate nature into their mediums. Get inspired. Now make your own vision.

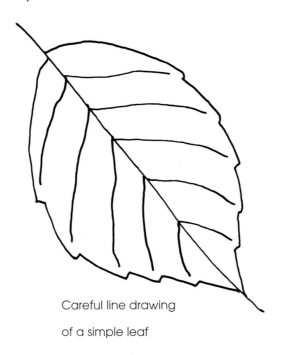

Careful line drawing

of a simple leaf

Approximating the edges with several straight lines

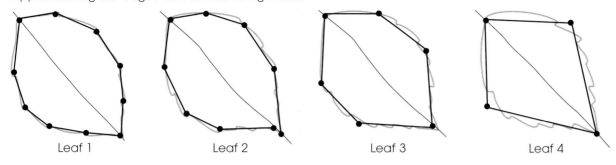

Leaf 1   Leaf 2   Leaf 3   Leaf 4

PREPARING A PIECING DIAGRAM FOR A BLOCK

From a large, detailed line drawing, you can begin the process of developing something that can be pieced. You will find that you cannot include every tiny part. As I work with this process, I find it becomes more a question of seeing how much I can leave out rather than how much I can put in.

WORKING FROM AN OUTLINE

Begin the process by placing tracing paper over your careful drawing, and then approximate the freely drawn outline (contour) of your subject with a series of straight lines. I begin the process by tracing the outline of the leaf on paper, then enlarging it when necessary on a copy machine to a more comfortable size.

Detail of *Black Beauty*, shown on page 8.

The resulting image can be pieced several ways. The blocks with Y seams will be much more difficult to sew by machine than the ones with y's, which are drawn by extending each edge line segment to the outside of the block. It is very helpful to make several progressively simpler versions of the pieced leaf before deciding which to use.

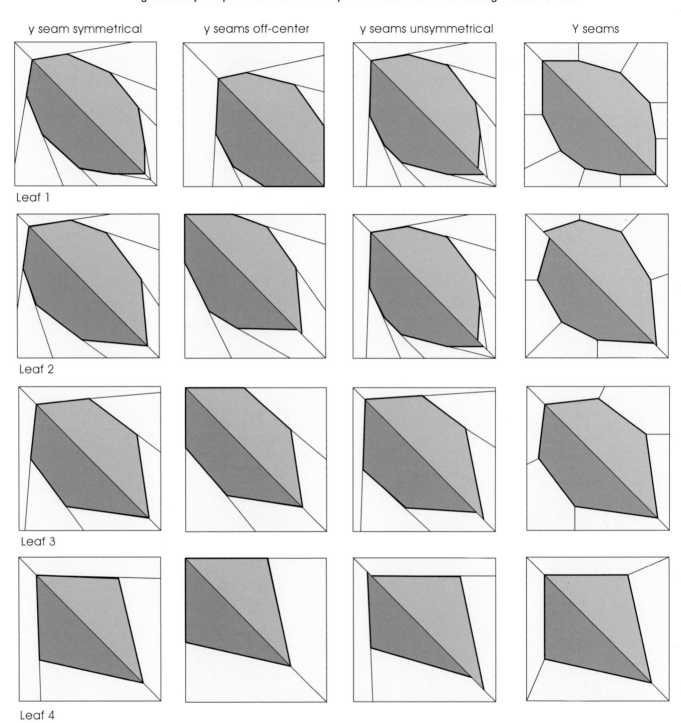

y seam symmetrical   y seams off-center   y seams unsymmetrical   Y seams

Leaf 1

Leaf 2

Leaf 3

Leaf 4

The last blocks are too clumsy in design for me, although they are the easiest to sew. The first block most closely approximates the leaf I began with, but have more templates than I care to use. The size of the block I will sew also influences my choice. If the block is enlarged to eight inches square, I could sew any of these leaves. With a three inch block, I would probably choose one of the middle versions. I have drawn the block with the main vein on the true diagonal, centering the leaf in the square. There are several other choices I might make.

GRAPH PAPER BLOCKS

Here, I have approximated the leaf on graph paper, using vertical, horizontal, or true diagonal angles. The arrows indicate the direction to press the seam allowance.

The vast majority of traditional quilt blocks use only these four directions for seaming. Ruby McKim's magnificent botanical designs from the thirties are drawn this way. Because this leaf block repeats the familiar squares, rectangles, and half-square triangles, this block will visually echo traditional patchwork. Compare the two of my quilts featuring foxgloves, *Foxgloves II* and *Rainy Day Dances* (both on the following page) for an interesting demonstration of piecing styles.

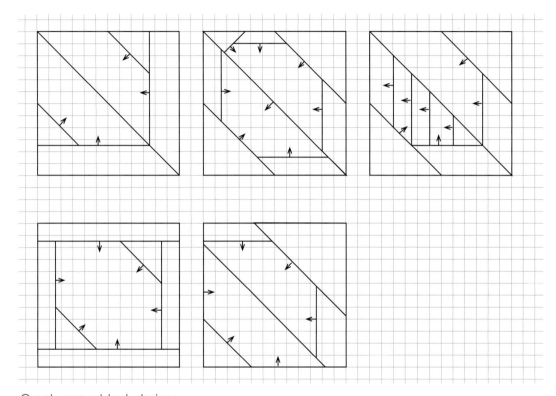

Graph paper block designs

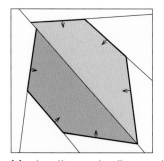

Detail of *Foxgloves II,* shown on page 158.   Detail of *Rainy Day Dances,* shown on page 56.

In *Foxgloves II*, the piecing is graph paper style. In *Rainy Day Dances*, the foxgloves are pieced with gently curved seams. I like both versions.

SLIDING THE DIAGONAL SEAM AWAY FROM THE CORNER

As mentioned earlier (page 42), a diagonal seam intersecting a corner makes joining the corners of several blocks a nuisance. By shifting the ends of the diagonal vein seam away from the corners, the block is easier to join and the leaf, visually, seems to have more movement. It tumbles.

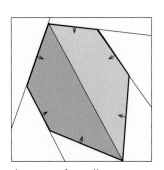
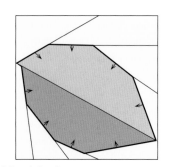
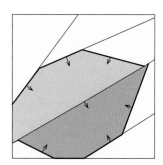

Moving the main diagonal vein away from the corner of the block

WORKING FROM A SKELETON

Rather than abstracting the leaf from the outline of the leaf, I can begin by working from the skeleton of the leaf.

On pieces of tracing paper laid over the leaf drawing, as we did with the outline of the leaf (on page 67), approximate the veins with a series of straight lines. Extend the seams as needed to make a pieceable block. Make several progressively simpler versions: first make a graph paper version, then repeat the process using gentle curves.

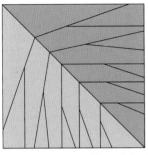  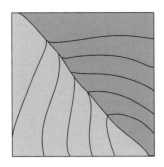 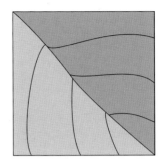

Pieced vein pattern blocks

These blocks can be used, as is, to piece a skeleton leaf. Or, add short line segments to make the leaf edge contour within the vein patterns (these edge lines may touch at the vein lines). If you want to make a serrated (toothed) leaf, mismatch the lines across the vein seam.

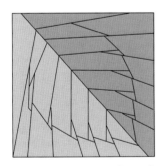   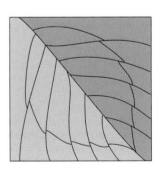

Adding edge contours to vein patterns by either matching contour line ends or mismatching them

The colors in a leaf are often slightly different between each pair of veins. Piecing leaves from a skeleton may result in a more natural color pattern. Each of these blocks depicts the leaf in a slightly different way. Choose the one that seems most appropriate to the specific leaf or project you have in mind.

OTHER COMBINATIONS

The halves of the various block patterns can obviously be combined to make more designs. For instance, combine straight with curved piecing, or combine edge contour leaves with skeleton leaves.

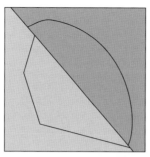 

Combining halves of curved and straight blocks

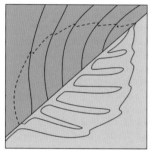  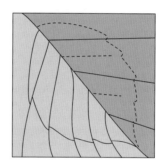 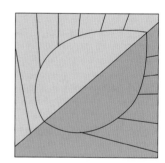

Combining edge contour designs with skeleton leaves

 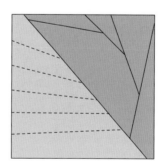

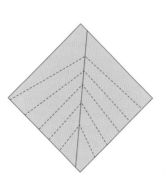  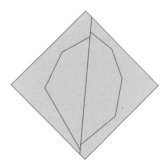

COMBINING PIECING AND APPLIQUÉ

Halves of any of the pieced blocks can also be combined with a half block made as an appliqué. Start by hand or machine appliquéing or reverse appliquéing half of a leaf to one triangle. Then sew it to a pieced half.

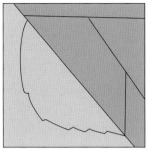

Half piecing and half appliqué

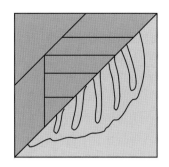

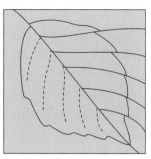

Half curved seam, with piecing along the vein pattern, and half appliqué

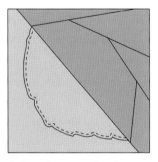

Soft-edge appliqué

Or use soft-edge appliqué to make half a leaf: Draw the contour edge of half a leaf onto fabric and layer it with a background fabric. Then stitch with a very small straight stitch along the contour edge. Trim the excess fabric close to the stitching with a small, sharp scissors. Using a very finely woven fabric for the leaf is recommended here to prevent excess fraying. (This is probably not a technique you will want to use on bed quilts.)

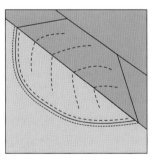

A leaf outlined with hoar frost

To make a leaf outlined with hoar frost, sandwich a piece of organza (cotton, silk, nylon, or metallic) between the leaf and background fabrics. Stitch the layers together. Trim the leaf fabric, then trim the organza, leaving it slightly wider in width.

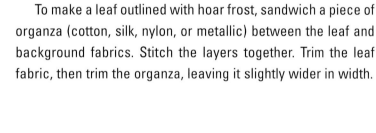

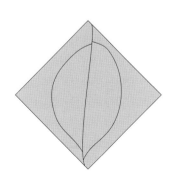

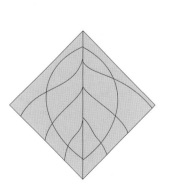

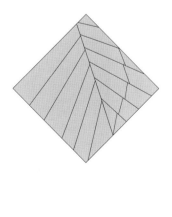

FLAPS

You might choose to make a slightly three-dimensional leaf by making one or both sides as a flap, or a faced flap. The faced flaps are sewn first, before the block is assembled.

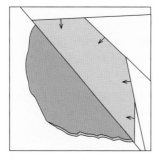 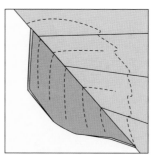

Leaves with flaps or faced flaps

Straight seam faced flaps combined with pieced veins and quilting

MAKING A FACED FLAP

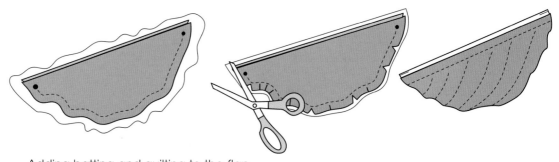

Cut two leaf halves, one right side up and one reversed, leaving ¼" seam allowances on all edges. With the leaf halves right sides together, sew the outer edge. This can be a simple smooth curve, a series of straight lines, or a more elaborate outline. Trim the seams and clip, if necessary. Turn the leaf right side out and press.

Lay the flap leaf on a piece of background fabric, matching the raw edges. Add the other half of the block, aligning the raw edges, and sew the seam through all layers. You can adjust the thickness of the flap by adding flannel, or batting, to the assembly process. If you want quilting stitches on the flap, sew these while the flap is still loose, before it is sewn into the block.

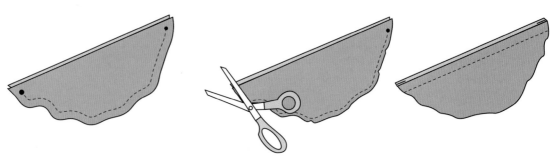

Adding batting and quilting to the flap

With the leaf halves right sides together, on top of the batting, stitch the outer seam through all layers. Trim and clip the curve. Trim the batting close to the seamline. Turn. Quilt through all layers.

Both the front and back of the leaf fabric can be cut from the same fabric, or you might use two different fabrics. (Leaves often have a different color or texture on the back from what you see on the front.) While the flap is still loose, use a technique from tailoring by using an iron to roll the outside seam edge slightly. A sliver of the backing will then show on the front, or a sliver of the front will show on the back.

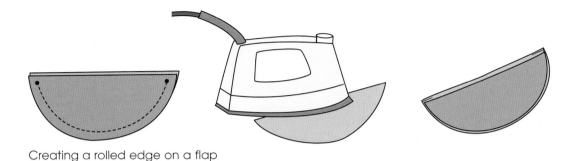

Creating a rolled edge on a flap

Sew the front to the backing, with right sides together. Trim and clip. Using a steam iron, roll the edge of the seam so a bit of the backing shows on the front of the leaf.

RUFFLES

Occasionally, one of the significant characteristics of a particular leaf or flower petal is some degree of ruffling. By adjusting the shape of a flap slightly, you can make a ruffle without using pleats or tucks.

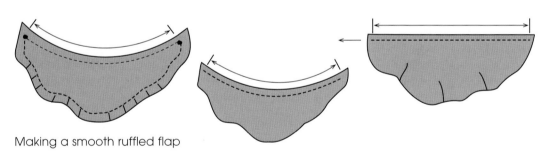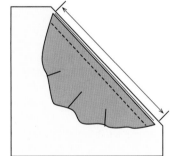

Making a smooth ruffled flap

Trace half the original leaf. To make a pattern for the ruffled flap, draw a curve the length of the original flap. (A shallow curve will make a slight ruffle, and a deep curve a fuller ruffle.) Redraw the outer edge of the leaf flap, matching the ends. Then make the flaps. Pull the ends to straighten the curve and pin the raw edges to the background piece. Stitch as usual.

These are a few of the options you might explore in your piecing. I'm sure you will find others.

The *Waterlilies* quilt employs several techniques: The back half of the flower is pieced into a block with curved seams and the petals at the front are faced then inserted in the seam along the bottom edge of the block, along with a folded piece of yellow fabric that is fringed to represent stamens. Also, the petals have collar stays placed inside them, which allow them to be adjusted individually.

Waterlilies

1985, 95" x 156"

machine pieced,

hand quilted, cottons,

cotton blends,

polyester batting

(artist's collection)

The upper half of each leaf is pieced into the quilt with a smooth curved seam. The lower half of each leaf is faced with burgundy fabric and caught in the seam at the center of the leaf. Most of the background is pieced in strips of varying widths, wider at the bottom and narrower at the top of the quilt. One fabric had a few scattered leaves on it that appear to float on the pond at the lower right, a happy accident from which I learned a lot.

Block Shapes

WORKING WITH THE GEOMETRY OF THE BLOCK

In the foregoing discussion, I have arbitrarily chosen a square for the shape of our pieced block. It is the block shape most often seen in traditional patchwork. There are, however, many other shapes that will work for pieced quilts.

Equilateral triangles (Thousand Pyramid quilts) and regular hexagons (Grandmother's Flower Garden quilts) are also shapes that will work. Any shape (tile) that will fit together with itself to cover a surface with no holes and no overlaps is said to tessellate. There are also pairs of shapes which will tessellate when used together (octagons and squares, for instance).

A few possible block shapes

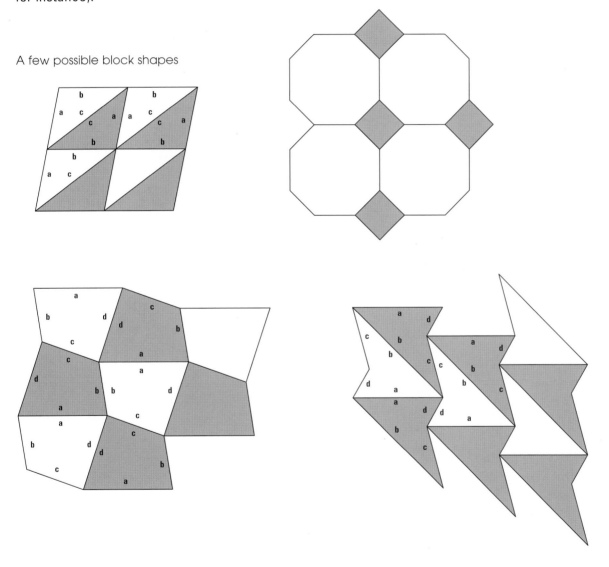

Look through geometry books, or make friends with a high-school geometry teacher, for ideas of the other tessellating shapes you might use for the shape of a quilt block. My favorite resource is a college text, *Tiling and Patterns*, by Grunbaum and Shepard. With it you could make quilts for the next several centuries, and never repeat the same design.

OTHER WAYS TO MAKE TESSELLATIONS

Tessellated blocks can also be derived by carefully deforming the sides of a regular grid, either by translation (sliding) or rotation (twisting).

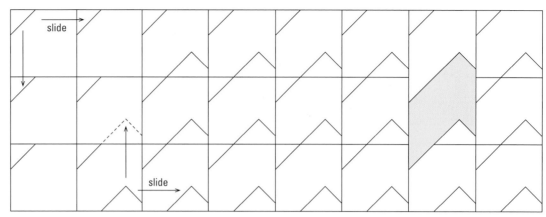

A simple tessellation by translation (sliding)

In the first example, I have made two changes to a grid of squares: First, I cut off the top left-hand corner, slid it across the block and added it to the top right-hand corner. Secondly, I took a bit out of the lower right corner and slid it to the top right-hand corner as well. The resulting block (tile) has six sides and is shaded at the right of the diagram.

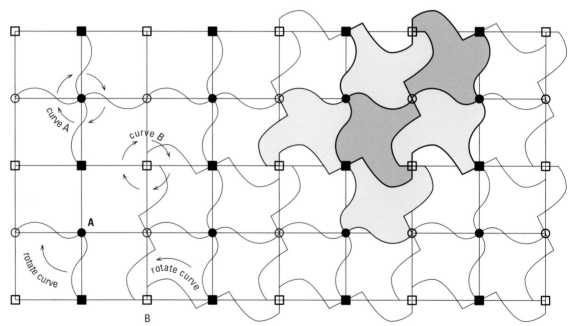

A simple tessellation by rotation

Beginning again with a grid of squares, I have drawn curve A, from point A in the center of a group of four squares. Curve A will replace one straight side of the first square. Then I have rotated curve A around point A, changing each straight side as I come to it. I've made this change at every A.

Moving to the intersections labeled B, I've drawn curve B to replace another straight side of the squares, rotating curve B around point B, and replacing the other four straight sides as I come to them. I've done this at every point B. The resulting block (tile) is shaded at the right side of the diagram.

As you can see, the blocks (tiles) fit together to cover the surfaces with no holes and no overlaps. They tessellate, but joining such blocks together in piecework will not be a simple process.

Here is one possibility to sew the block from the simple tesselation: Make half of the blocks in Colorway 1 and half in Colorway 2. Then join the square blocks as in a checkerboard.

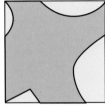
Colorway 1

Colorway 2

You may, in fact, find it easier to assemble all of the elements in the original square grid, then sew the resulting square blocks together. There are many sources of instruction about this process, which can become complicated indeed. M.C. Escher was the master of the tessellation process. Some of these tessellations are practical for piecework. Others are very cumbersome to sew in fabric.

Pines at Twilight
1987, 43.5" x 41.5"
machine pieced,
machine and hand
quilted, cotton blends,
cotton-polyester batting
(private collection)

YET ANOTHER WAY TO MAKE TESSELLATED BLOCKS

Rather than beginning with a grid, it is possible to design a tessellation by beginning with a single figure; in this case, a radish.

Radish sketch

Straight-line piecing version

After making multiple copies of the straight-line version, I experimented with various configurations until I found one I liked. Then I taped the copies together in a regular way.

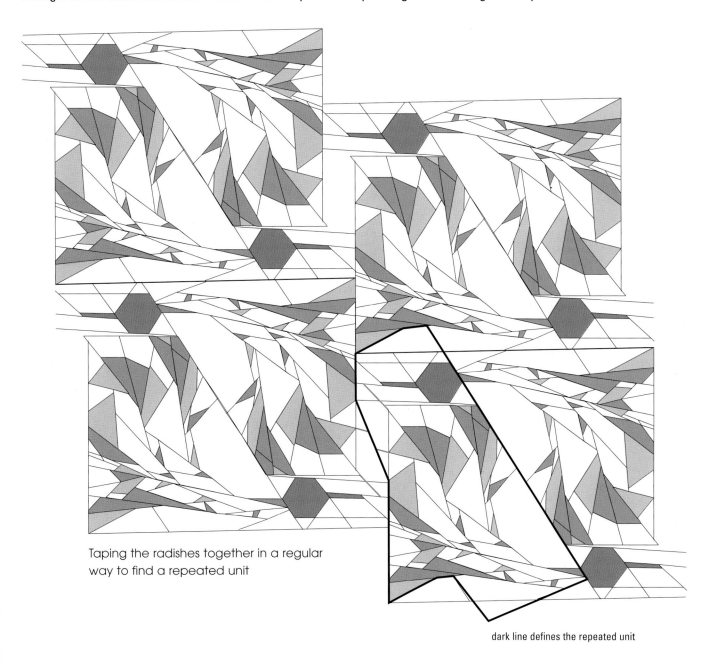

Taping the radishes together in a regular way to find a repeated unit

dark line defines the repeated unit

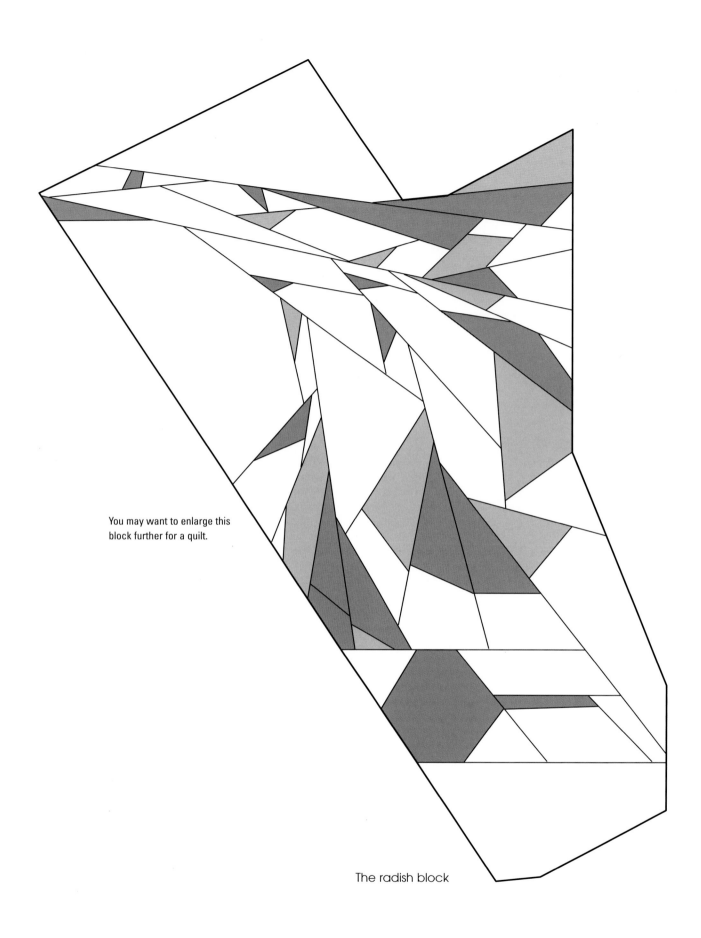

You may want to enlarge this block further for a quilt.

The radish block

By carefully following the lines, and with very few changes, I was able to find a unit that repeated to form this pattern. When made in multiples and joined together, this "block" will produce the arrangement of a radish quilt.

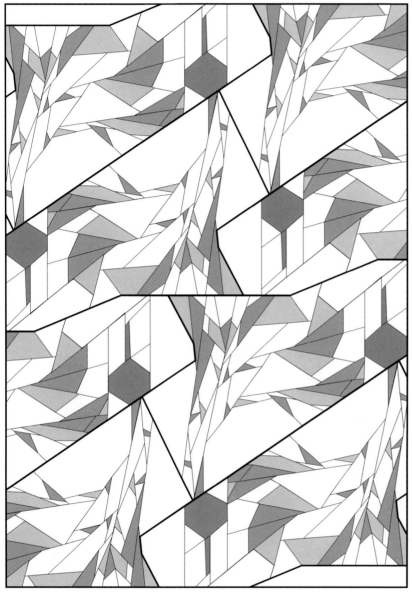

Radish quilt

In making a quilt of this kind, I cut all the templates for the pieces, string piecing (see page 8) all of the blocks at once (joining the first piece to the second piece for all of the blocks). When all the blocks are finished, I join the block units together; in this case, with many short seams.

Geometry

WORKING WITH THE GEOMETRY OF THE SUBJECT MATTER

Sometimes there will be a clear geometric structure to a plant or animal which can suggest a geometry to use for a block. I used the symmetry of the three-part arrowhead flower as a starting point for the *Arrowhead* quilt. This suggested that the design for the quilt be based on equilateral triangles. When I introduced the concept of graph-paper design for the arrowhead, I drew the quilt on equilateral triangle graph paper (a graph paper where three sets of gridlines cross at 60°). There are quilt sources and engineering sources of equilateral triangle paper, or you can draft your own by hand or with a home computer.

The seamlines I've drawn are all either parallel to or perpendicular to one of the lines of the triangle paper.

Arrowhead

1985, 51" x 45"

machine pieced,

machine and hand

quilted, cotton,

cotton blends,

polyester batting

(private collection)

Several years ago, I tried many block versions of a butterflyweed, a five-part flower with upper and lower sections, placed within a five-sided regular pentagon. As I looked at the flower from the top, I could come up with a piecing plan, but lost the upper and lower aspect of the flower.

Abandoning pentagons, I found I could use a regular hexagon, and by viewing the flower from the side, draw the upper part of the flower in one hexagon and the lower part in an adjacent hexagon. Hexagons, and pairs of hexagons, tessellate, and the entire quilt was planned around the clusters of hexagonal flower blocks.

Butterflyweed
1987, 77" x 96"
machine pieced,
hand quilted, cottons,
cotton blends,
polyester batting
(private collection)

Lesson: You don't have to put a five-part flower in a five-part block, nor must you put the center of the flower in the center of the block.

Piecing Complicated Quilts

When embarking to make a quilt from a full-size drawing, you will have to organize how you will keep track of the pieces, fabrics, templates, and sewing order. The scale of the problem will become more difficult than your memory will be able to manage alone.

ENLARGING DRAWINGS

If your drawing is smaller than the size you would like to use for the finished quilt, there are several ways to enlarge it.

1. You can draw a proportionately larger image.

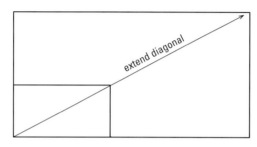

For one method of drawing the same proportion at a larger size, first draw a diagonal line on the small original rectangle. Then extend this diagonal line outside the rectangle. The diagonals of all proportional rectangles will be along this line.

For another proportional enlargement method mark the center, horizontally and vertically, of both the small drawing and the new larger one. Sketch freehand onto the larger paper from the smaller drawing, working with one quarter of the image at a time.

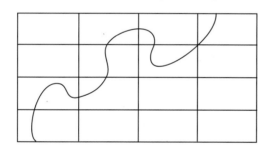

Or, draw a grid on the small drawing and the same grid on the larger proportion. Copy the elements in each box of the grid on the small drawing into the boxes on the larger drawing.

2. You can project the image onto a wall at the size you need using an opaque projector (you may be able to borrow one from a school or library). Trace the projected image.

3. Take a slide of the drawing. With a slide projector, focus the slide on the wall at the size needed. Trace the projected image.

4. Take the drawing to a copy center. Many copiers have an enlargement function. Some can copy onto 11" x 17" or larger paper. Large copy centers often have machines that run paper from rolls 36" wide. To enlarge greater than 200%, you may have to work in steps, making the first copy as large as you can, then enlarging that copy, until you reach the desired size. For a very large drawing, you may have to cut it into strips or sections and enlarge each section separately, then tape them together.

Once you have a drawing of the size required for the quilt, proceed to making the template drawing.

Note: DO NOT CUT THE TEMPLATE DRAWING UP ENTIRELY. CUT EACH SECTION AS YOU USE IT.

CHOOSING A PAPER FOR THE TEMPLATE DRAWING

Decide whether you wish to use vellum, freezer paper, or some other material for the paper templates from which you will cut each piece of fabric.

Vellum

PROS

I use vellum (a 16 lb. heavy-weight tracing paper) from an architect/engineering/art supply source. You can find vellum in sheets, pads, or rolls, with plain or with an 8-to-the-inch light blue grid. The paper is stiff enough to trace around and I use it for templates. It is strong and very tough, and can survive many erasures. The blue grid enables me to square up edges, to construct vertical and horizontal elements accurately, and to orient the direction of the prints or plaids precisely.

Vellum is very transparent, allowing for easy tracing and for careful placement on patterned fabrics. I can see through the paper to select a particular part of the design for each template. Also, vellum comes in large sizes, up to 42 inches wide by 20 yards long.

CONS

Vellum is not inexpensive. A 24" wide roll, 20 yards long, costs about 50¢ per foot, which is less costly than plastic or Mylar®, but more costly than freezer paper. Vellum is not as readily available in every locality. Vellum cannot be "ironed on", but can be pinned to fabric pieces, or perhaps stuck with a temporary glue-stick adhesive.

Freezer Paper

Some students trace their designs on freezer paper and cut up the freezer paper drawing to use as templates.

PROS

Freezer paper is easily obtainable in grocery stores or quilt shops. Freezer paper can be traced through. The templates can be ironed onto fabric after they are cut out, and left attached to the fabric pieces until they are sewn, making it easier to keep track of them. Freezer paper sticks to the fabric and is easily traced around, doesn't injure the fabric, and can be peeled off and reused several times if fabric choices change. Freezer paper is relatively inexpensive.

CONS

Freezer paper is not as transparent as vellum, making it difficult to see through and place precisely on a patterned fabric. Freezer paper usually does not have a printed grid on it, making it more difficult to square off a quilt or to find precise horizontals and verticals. Freezer paper is not particularly strong. Freezer paper is sometimes difficult to erase marks on.

Quilting teachers usually suggest that a design be traced on the dull, non-plasticized side of freezer paper. This presents two problems for my students: If the freezer-paper templates are ironed on to the right side of the fabric, the fabrics are not visible if pinned to the wall prior to sewing. Also, if the freezer paper is ironed on the wrong side of the fabric, the pieces can be pinned to the wall so the fabric shows, but the entire drawing will be reversed when sewn together. Some can get used to that reversal; others simply find it too confusing.

I suggest that the design be traced onto the shiny, plasticized side of freezer paper. This can be done with a permanent marker or a sharp pencil. A permanent marker may be preferred to a pencil because the tic marks along curved seams will be easier to see. But, be aware that some markers may transfer a slight image to very light fabrics. Mark the tics along the seam lines on the dull side of the freezer paper as well as any identifying piecing codes.

The freezer-paper templates can then be ironed onto the wrong side of the fabrics, and left on the fabric pieces as they are pinned up for visual inspection. Mark the sewing line with pencil by tracing around the freezer-paper piece on the back of each fabric piece. Mark the tics in the seam allowance. Cut the fabric pieces 1/4" larger than the paper piecing. The image is sewn as shown in the original drawing, not reversed.

If the piecing is done by machine with straight seams, the freezer paper can even be left on the back of the fabric pieces, when sewing along the edge of the paper for a seam line. If piecing curved seams, make sure to trace around the edge of the freezer-paper pieces, and mark all tic marks. Remove the paper before sewing, so that you can manipulate the fabric pieces as needed for the curved seams.

Other Materials

You may find some other material that you prefer to use. Quilters are remarkably inventive. Some have found that they like to work with a supply of drafting Mylar, which has become obsolete at engineering firms that have switched to computer-drawn images. Mylar is wonderful stuff, but normally it is rather expensive. Find something that works for you and your budget.

ORIENTATION

You will probably want to invent some system that will help you remember where each template/fabric piece goes in your design. Some designs break easily into large sections, and these can be numbered and lettered as I did in *Horn Pond 2* (page 124). One student drew colored lines across both drawing and template tracing before it was cut up. Each cut paper template could then be matched to the other templates and the drawing by matching the colored lines.

You will almost certainly want to write a few notes on the drawing and the template drawing: light, medium, dark, stone, water, tree trunk, barn, hill 1 or 2 or 3, or perhaps even a color name or texture suggestion.

GETTING STARTED

With the drawing on the wall and template drawing prepared, I begin the fabric selection by looking at my fabric stash, pulling out fabrics that seem to be possibilities.

When I find a fabric that seems like a good choice, I fold it to about the size I need, and pin the folded fabric to the drawing on the wall. I repeat this process, selecting fabrics for other places, and stand back to contemplate how well they work.

This process will gradually help me resolve my choice of fabric selection. Sometimes the fabric choices reflect pretty closely the image from which I'm working. Other times, a particular fabric will attract my attention and suggest a very different direction.

As soon as I feel fairly sure of one or two fabrics, I take down the folded pieces, cut out their paper templates, trace the templates on the back of the selected fabrics, cut them out, and pin the fabric pieces back on the drawing on the wall, saving the paper templates so I can find them to reuse if necessary. After using each paper template, tape them back together, or put them in plastic bags. Find a system so that you can find the proper template if you change your mind later and wish to select a different fabric.

MARKING FROM THE PAPER TEMPLATES

Having selected a fabric and ironed it if necessary, I lay the fabric down on a flat surface wrong side up. Sometimes I use a cutting board or a piece of sandpaper or the ironing board for this part. I put the paper template wrong side up on the back of the fabric, sticking pins through the paper into the fabric, if possible, to hold it in place.

Or, if using the freezer-paper templates prepared as I have suggested, put the freezer-paper piece shiny side down on the back of the fabric, and iron it so that the freezer-paper sticks to the fabric.

With a pencil of a color that I can easily see, I trace a line around the edge of the paper template. This pencil line, on the back of the cloth, will be the sewing line. You will want to be able to find this line easily in the cutting, pinning, and piecing process. If a graphite pencil won't show up enough, I use a colored pencil, choosing whatever color will show on that particular fabric. The marks are on the back of the fabric, not the front where they might show on the quilt.

Happy Birthday
1995, 49" x 37"
machine pieced,
machine quilted,
cottons,
cotton batting
(artist's collection)

TICS

Any seams, straight or curved, will join more precisely when you mark and pin the end-points of both pieces before you begin to sew. In very complicated quilts, with many of the fabrics off-grain, this is especially important. Crosswise grains stretch more than length-wise grains, and different fabrics stretch at different rates.

In my complicated pieces, I make tic marks at every intersection or end of a seam and at intervals along it. With tight curves, the tics may be one inch apart; gentle curves two inches apart, and long straight edges four inches apart. Each tic is marked in the seam allowance on the wrong side of the fabric with a pencil that I will be able to see. When joining two seams, I make sure that each pair of tic marks matches along the seam and at the endpoints. I carefully pin each set together, removing the pins just before the needle reaches them.

CUTTING FROM THE PAPER TEMPLATES

When the outline of the paper templates has been traced on the wrong side of a piece of fabric, and all of the tics are marked as well, I cut out the piece leaving 1/4" seam outside the traced sewing line. At this point I can estimate a 1/4" seam more accurately than I can mark it. Some students mark a 1/4" seam allowance outside the traced seamline with a quilter's ruler or other device. The sewing will be done along the traced, penciled sewing line.

Since most of my pieces are very odd shapes, I do my cutting with a pair of scissors. Some students prefer to use a rotary cutter.

If I am using freezer paper for templates, I leave the freezer paper attached to the back of each piece at this point. If I am not using freezer paper for templates, I tape the paper templates back together after I use each one, gradually reconstructing the template drawing as I go.

Find a method that works for you and use it.

SEWING

After choosing, marking, and cutting, I pin each piece of fabric is pinned back on the drawing on the wall. When fabrics for a convenient section have all been selected and cut, I carefully consider which is the most logical order in which to sew them together.

Carefully taking the pieces of fabric down two by two, I piece them, right sides together with a 1/4" seam on my sewing machine, sewing along the penciled lines and pinning as needed.

If there are curves or inset corners, I clip as needed before I sew. If there are puzzle pieces, I may leave some parts of seams open and finish them later. See the technical directions for curved seams (on pages 12-18), insets (on pages 20-31), and puzzle pieces (on pages 33-35) in Part 1.

PRESSING

After sewing each seam, I determine the direction I want to press and then press with a steam iron. As the piecing continues, sections are gradually joined together until the top is complete.

CHANGING FABRIC PIECES

If I decide to change the fabric in a piece that is already sewn, I remove the offending piece with a seam ripper, find its paper template, mark and cut a new piece with the new fabric, and sew the new piece by machine where I removed the old one.

New World Tree
1997, 72" x 90"
machine pieced,
machine quilted,
cottons,
cotton batting
(artist's collection)

St. Johnswort

I will use a lovely large-scale photograph of a St. Johnswort from *New Zealand Alpine Plants, Inside and Out*, by Bill and Nancy Malcolm, as the starting point for my first demonstration of piecing a design.

To begin, I make a detailed tracing of the photo and, if necessary, enlarge the line drawing to a larger size from which it is easier to work. Working on a design at the size I intend to sew helps me determine exactly how much simplification I need to do to make a pieceable design. Making a line drawing first makes it a little easier for you to see the contours of your subject.

With this flower, there are several different ways I could begin the planning. This St. Johnswort flower has five fairly simple petals and five sepals when viewed from the front. I can also see stamens, anthers, and the ovaries bursting from the center.

A St. Johnswort flower

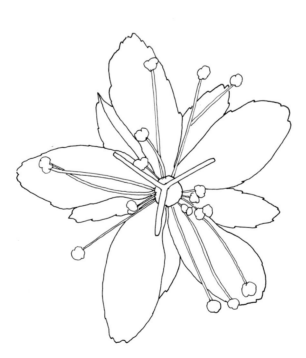

Careful tracing of a St. Johnswort blossom

Approximating St. Johnswort petals and sepals with straight-line segments

For the first design, I will ignore the smaller parts, and begin with the outline of the petals and sepals. Working from the outline, I have approximated the edge with short straight line segments, as we did with the simple leaf in the preceding section.

Extending some of the lines to make the piecing diagram suggests that I need about 48 templates. Note that I have left the resolution of the center undefined at the moment. Like the flower, the design radiates from the center. It could be pieced in ten radial wedges (labeled A through J in the block).

I've colored the petals yellow and the sepals green to help you discern the pattern. The background pieces that complete the rectangular block can be any fabrics you desire. I like to vary the fabrics slightly so that adjacent background pieces are different colors to show off the piecing. The pieces in each wedge are numbered in the sewing order for that wedge (the exception is wedge D: Sew 1 to 2; sew 3 to 4, 5, and 6; then sew 1,2 to 3,4,5,6).

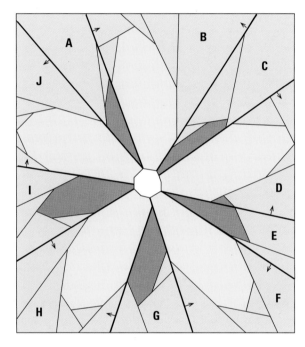

St. Johnswort block, straight-line piecing, 48 templates, center unresolved

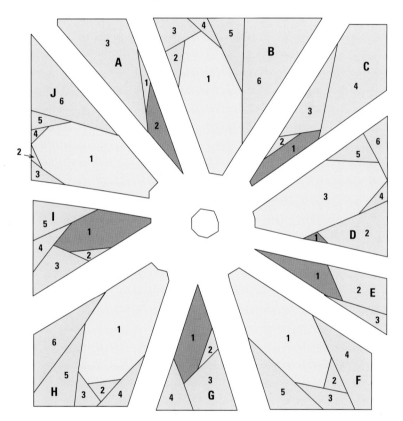

I can make a simpler block by reducing the number of line segments in the outline edges. This time I have about 38 pieces, and, again, a design of ten radiating wedges. I've left the center unresolved as we did in the block on page 93.

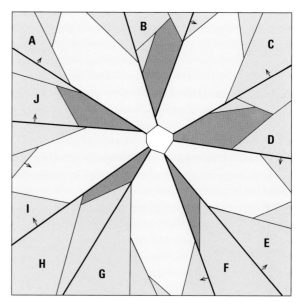

St. Johnswort block, straight-line piecing, 38 templates, center unresolved

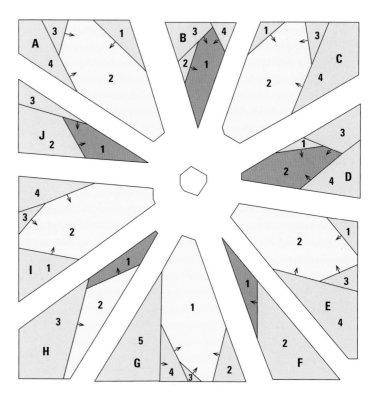

As I sew the block together I carefully consider the direction in which I press the seam allowance of each seam. Pressing the seams under the flower parts, as shown with the small arrows, will make the flower stand out from the background. This can enhance the low relief of the quilting stitches, especially when the quilting stitches outline the flower just outside the ditch.

The intersection of many seams at the center of the flower can be handled several ways. If I bring all the seams to a central point, I will have a piecing nightmare. I could stop all the seams slightly short of the center and appliqué or reverse appliqué a patch in the center hole.

For a flower with a raised center, like a daisy, an appliquéd center would be appropriate. For a flower with a depressed center, like a morning glory, a reverse appliqué will let the center recede. If I am very careful, I can piece by hand or machine a little angular center like the one in the block on page 94.

In working out a piecing solution for the center of the block, I will use some of the tricks from the simple leaf. Arranging a piecing diagram so that the ends of the seams are offset from each other with some seams ending slightly before they get to the center is a good solution to eliminate bulk.

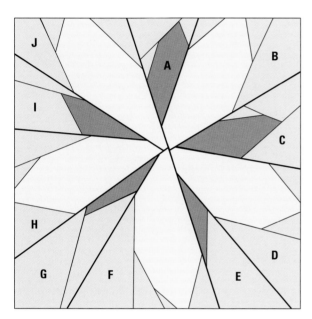

A straight-line pieced block that is easy to sew,
one seam joins the two parts of the block together

For a radial design such as the one above, I may be able to avoid Y seams at the center if I can find one seam that can be shifted slightly so that it runs all the way through the block, dividing it in two parts.

Using the radial block (on page 95), I can now add a center with little wedges sewn to the five petal pieces, either with five small templates or by a sew-and-flip-technique (page 48). To make the center slightly raised, I will press these seam allowances toward the center and away from the petals.

Notice that the ends of these wedges are staggered slightly, and that two wedges interrupt the central circle. This loose design complements the slightly asymmetrical design of the petals in this block, and keeps the flower looking informal and organic, rather than making it look like a target.

Sew in wedges; sew A, B, C, D, E, F, G, H, I, J. Sew A to B; C to D to E; F to G; H to I to J; then sew AB to CDE; HIJ to FG; and sew ABCDE to FGHIJ.

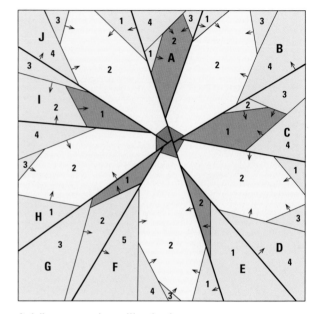

Adding a center with piecing

The little bits in the center are a good location for a tiny bright shot of color to bring the flower to life. Use whatever color pleases you (raspberry, orange, bright blue, chartreuse, black) rather than literally following your subject's center. All five bits can be the same, or different, whichever you choose.

Here's a simplification of the preceding block, this time approximating the edges of the petals and sepals with even fewer straight lines. This version is certainly easier to sew than the preceding one. However, some of the character of this particular St. Johnswort is lost with this design.

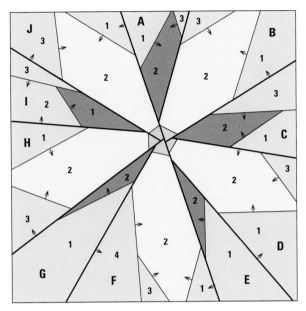

Sew in wedges; sew A to B, C to D to E, F to G, H to I to J; then sew AB to CDE, FG to HIJ; and sew ABCDE to FGHIJ.

St. Johnswort block, 29 pieces plus the center; use a sew-and-flip-technique, or use small triangle template

I can repeat this process using smooth curved seams rather than straight seams, as we did with the simple leaf. I try to approximate the contours of the flower with curves that I know I can sew: that is, curves of a gentle radius.

Smooth curve approximation of the St. Johnswort petals and sepals

A pieced block from curved seams can be as simple as shown in the block below. Note that I have one smooth curve that goes all the way through the block and that I have drawn the seams so they fall in slightly different places in the center. Add tic marks (registration marks) to your pattern, marking the tics along the seamlines on the back of each piece of fabric. Tics should be placed at every intersection and every inch or two along each seam. When joining the pieces, clip the seam allowance on the concave edge as necessary and pin the corresponding tics together. Five small templates or sew-and-flip center pieces are added to each petal piece as in the previous blocks.

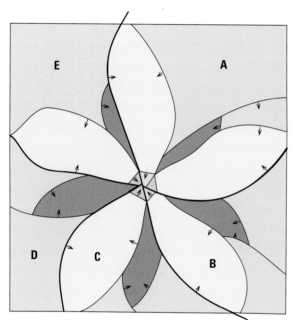

Curved seam pieced St. Johnswort block.

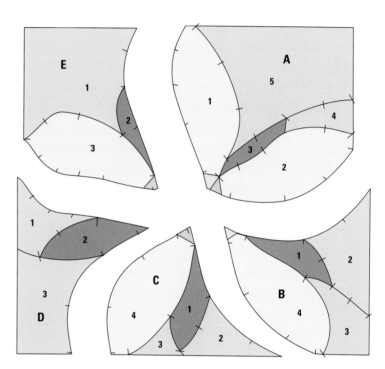

Add tic marks to all curved seams, and clipping all concave edges, begin the sewing process. For section A, add centers to petals 1 and 2. Sew 3 to 4 to 5; sew 3,4,5 to 2; and then sew 1 to 2,3,4,5. Press seam allowances in the direction of the arrow. For section B, add a center to petal 4. Sew 1 to 2 to 3 to 4. For section C, sew a center to petal 4. Sew 1 to 2 to 3 to 4. For section D, sew 1 to 2 to 3. For section E, add a center to petal 3. Sew 1 to 2 to 3. Sew A to B; C to D to E; then sew AB to CDE.

It is often the case that you will need fewer templates with a curved seam design than you will need for straight-line piecing. Curved seams are a little more difficult to sew and more time consuming. The visual character of a curved-seam pieced block is different than the character of a straight-seam pieced block. Compare these blocks (pages 98 and 99) with the previous blocks (pages 94–97). In some subjects, such as calla lilies, the curve is of such importance to the character of the plant that a curved seam solution may be best. But because of the physical limits of curved seam sewing (fairly gentle curves), the undulations of curved seams can sometimes become almost cartoonish.

Straight-seam piecing generally looks more energetic and dynamic. It is simpler piecing and can incorporate the sew-and-flip technique more easily. Straight seams relate in character to traditional patchwork blocks. They sometimes have a more abstract quality. Draw both curved and straight blocks and consider the visual differences between them before you choose which to use.

Seams in center of petals and stamens can be pressed to either side or pressed open.

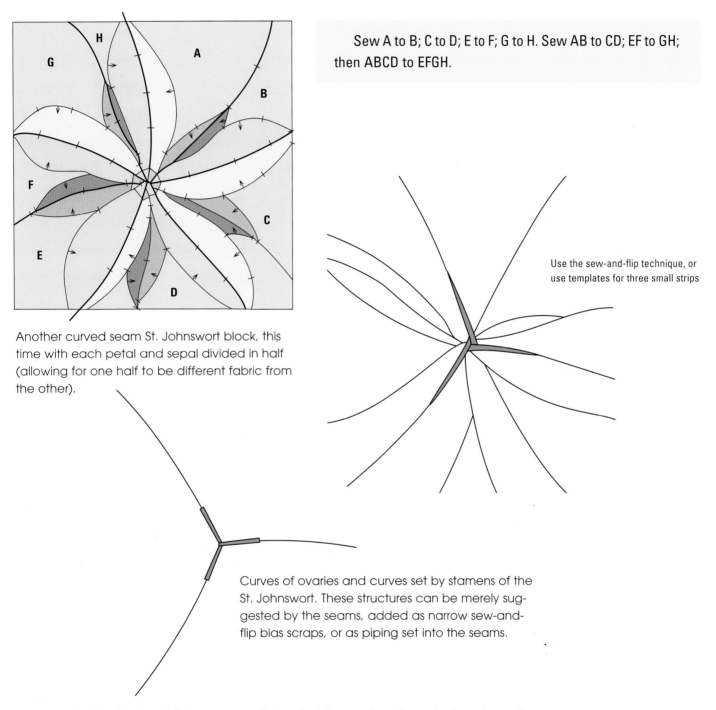

Sew A to B; C to D; E to F; G to H. Sew AB to CD; EF to GH; then ABCD to EFGH.

Another curved seam St. Johnswort block, this time with each petal and sepal divided in half (allowing for one half to be different fabric from the other).

Use the sew-and-flip technique, or use templates for three small strips

Curves of ovaries and curves set by stamens of the St. Johnswort. These structures can be merely suggested by the seams, added as narrow sew-and-flip bias scraps, or as piping set into the seams.

Instead of beginning with the contours (edges) of the petals and sepals, I can focus first on the ovary and stamen structure at the center. The ovary has three branches, and I have begun the sketch by drawing those lines first. I've extended them to make them the focal point of the design, then sketched in the curves set up by the stamens.

In adding the petals and sepals to the block (on page 99), I have broken their edges slightly as they cross the lines of the previous drawing. This puts the petals and sepals slightly out of focus, so they do not overwhelm the structure of the center parts.

Add tic marks, and clipping all concave edges, begin the sewing process. Sew in wedges A–M in three groups. The first group is ABC, the second group is DEFH, and the third group is IJKLM. Sew A to B to C; add strip 1; then sew D to E to F, G to H to DEF; and add strip 2. Sew J to K to L; sew I and M to JKL, and add strip 3. Within the block, there is one Y seam right in the middle. Join the three groups together with the Y seam, stopping right at the center and backstitching the ends of these seams.

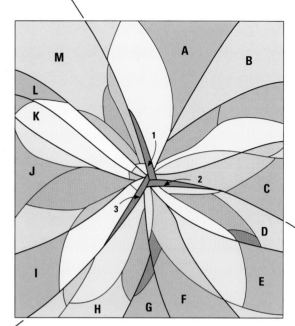

Curved seam St. Johnswort block, focused on center parts, with petals and sepals fractured.

Here's an alternative drawing, made this time with straight seams. I might add beads to the stamen seams as an extra detail.

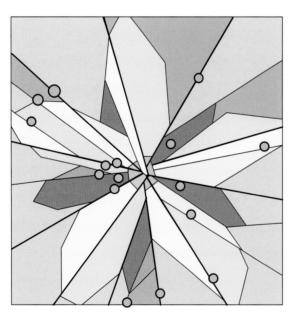

Straight-seam St. Johnswort block, focused on center parts, Y seam at the center.

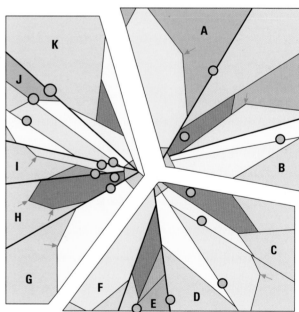

Sew in wedges; sew A to B. Sew C to D to E to F; sew G to H to I to J to K; sew Y seam to join sections. (Arrows indicate inset corners.)

Another characteristic of the St. Johnswort is a very unusual defense to protect this alpine plant from being overgrazed by animals. There is a slightly notched edge to the petals, sepals, and leaves, and a very tiny black dot at each of these notches. The dot is a cell structure containing a poisonous pigment.

Here's another straight-seam design, in which the slightly notched edge of one half of each petal is developed by the piecing. I've left out the notches on the other side of each petal and on the sepals to keep the design from becoming too complicated. I might sew a tiny black bead just inside each notch. Because I have divided the petal into sections to make the notches, I have the option of using many different fabrics in this block.

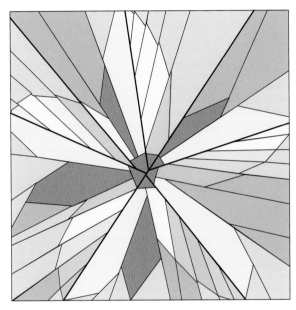

St. Johnswort block showing the edge defenses

Sew in wedges; sew A to B to C; sew E to F to G; sew D to EFG; and sew the two halves together.

With all of the preceding designs, I have worked with the slight irregularity of the flower as you see it in nature. I can also begin a design by emphasizing the geometric structure on which the flower is based. St. Johnswort belongs to the class of flowering plants that have five petals and five sepals. You may occasionally find an odd one with four or six petals, but that is an aberration, just as four-leafed clovers are a rarity in a patch of the usual three-leafed ones.

For this design I have begun with a regular pentagon, which has five equal sides and five equal angles. In one of the five triangles that are enclosed in the pentagon, I have drawn one fifth of a flower. The petals (and sepals) exhibit mirror symmetry, so I have drawn one half of one petal as the mirror image of the other. I can piece this geometric flower by making five of these triangles and joining them together, with a small triangular template, a sew-and-flip triangle, or with a small appliquéd pentagon as a center.

I can divide this pattern in several ways. In the version 1 block (page 103), there is a seam in the center of each petal (giving you the option of shading the two sides of each petal differently). I could divide the pentagon though the middle of each sepal, leaving the petals whole as in the version 2 block, or through the middles of both petals and sepals, or by shifting the end of one seam slightly as in the version 3 block, splitting the piecing to include one whole petal and sepal in each subunit.

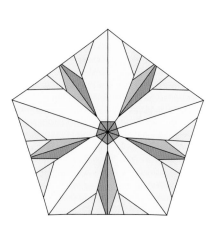

Geometric version of a St. Johnswort block constructed in a regular pentagon

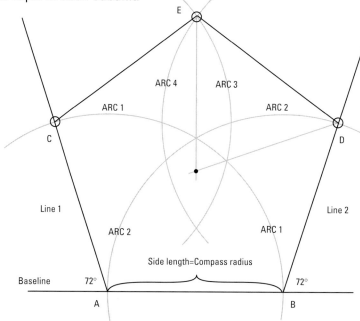

To draw a regular pentagon: Draw a baseline, then set the compass to a desired side length, place the compass pin at point A and draw: Where arc 1 crosses the baseline is point B.

Move the compass to point B and draw arc 2. With a good protractor, draw line 1 at a 72° angle to the baseline at points A and B. Point C is the intersection of line 1 and arc 1; point D is the intersection of line 1 and arc 2.

With the compass pin at point C, draw arc 3. With the compass pin at point D, draw arc 4. Where arc 3 and arc 4 cross at the top is point E, the top of the pentagon: Connect C to E and D to E.

ALTERNATIVE WAYS OF ASSEMBLING A GEOMETRIC ST. JOHNSWORT BLOCK

For version 1, sew five of these triangles (seam in center of petals). For version 2, sew five of these units (seam in center of sepal). For version 3, sew five of these units (petal and sepal in each unit).

In all of these versions, very few templates are required because each template is used five times.

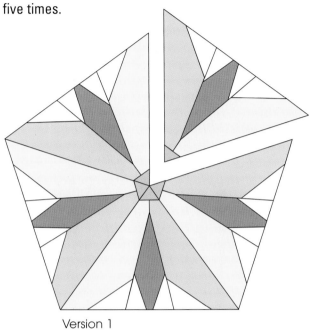

Version 1

Version 2

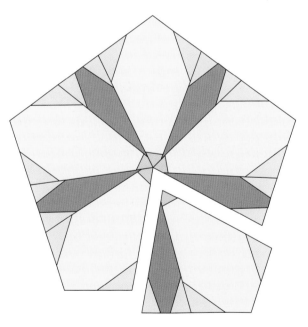

Version 3 - The center of this version can vary, depending on the sewing order.

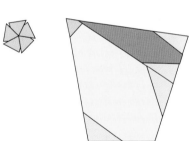

center triangle added to petal before sepal

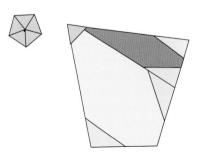

center triangle added to petal after sepal

Regular pentagons will not tessellate. That is, they will not cover the surface of your quilt with no holes and no overlaps, unless you combine them with a particular small diamond. The sides of the diamond are the same length as the sides of the pentagon, and the angles of the opposite corners are 36° and 144°. The tessellation of pentagons and diamonds is a very interesting one, and can be arranged either symmetrically or almost randomly. I can use pentagons with pieced flowers, and pentagons of a single piece of fabric, along with the diamonds, if I choose. Of course, the pentagons do not all need to be made of pieced flowers. Some could be solid pieces of fabric, others pieced in a simpler way.

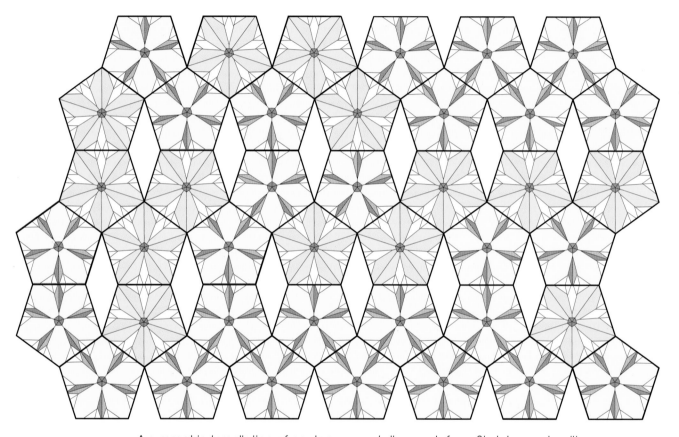

A symmetric tessellation of pentagons and diamonds for a St. Johnswort quilt

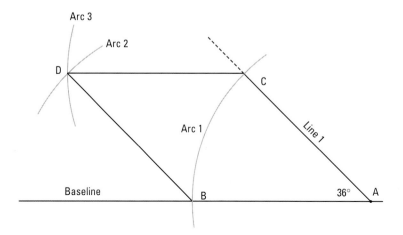

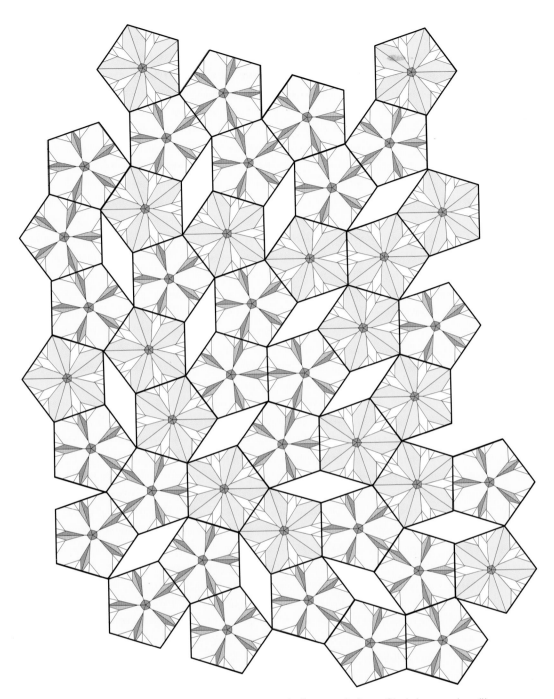

An unsymmetric tessellation of pentagons and diamonds for a St. Johnswort quilt.

To construct the diamond (same side length as the pentagon, page 102): Draw a baseline. Set the compass to the length of the side of the pentagon. Place the compass pin at A. Draw arc 1, where arc 1 crosses the baseline is point B; then with a protractor, draw line 1 at a 36° angle to the baseline at point A. Where line 1 crosses arc 1 is point C. Put the compass pin at B and draw arc 2. Put the compass pin at C and draw arc 3; the intersection of arc 2 and arc 3 is point D. Connect BD and CD.

There is another type of pentagon that will tessellate in a very particular way. This one also has five sides of the same length, but the angles between the sides are different. The "squashed" pentagon contains mirror symmetry along the center line, so a block could be planned in which the templates are used twice (once reversed).

"Squashed" tessellating pentagon block, its construction and arrangement.

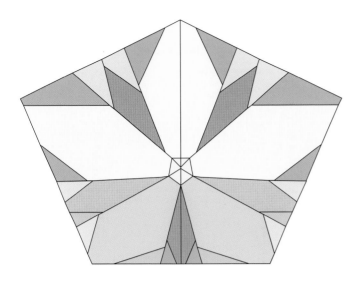

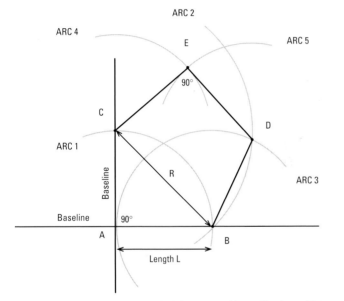

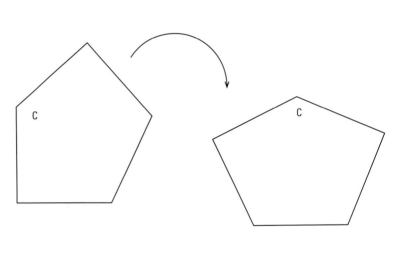

Squashed Pentagon, all sides equal length, two 90° angles

Draw two baselines at 90° on graph paper. Set an accurate compass to side length L. With the pin of the compass at A, draw arc 1 (points B and C will be where arc 1 crosses the baselines). Reset the compass to length R (C to B). With the pin at C, draw arc 2. Reset the compass to side length L. With the pin at B, draw arc 3 to find point D. Set the pin at C, and draw arc 4. Set the pin at D, and draw arc 5 to find point E. Connect BD, CE, and DE.

ARRANGING THE BLOCKS

These figures have exploited a single flower, face on, to make pieced block designs. The blocks themselves can then be arranged several different ways.

If I adapt any of the St. Johnswort figures to fit in a square block, I have more possibilities. With the square blocks, I can make quilts like the ones shown.

Several arrangements of St. Johnswort blocks

Make eight blocks and one center block.

Make three blocks.

The addition of sashing strips and borders, each of which is also pieced with curves is shown with the rectangular blocks.

Make twelve square blocks.

Square blocks having four equal sides can be rotated randomly as they are set together. Placing the flower off-center in the block will exaggerate the block's randomness.

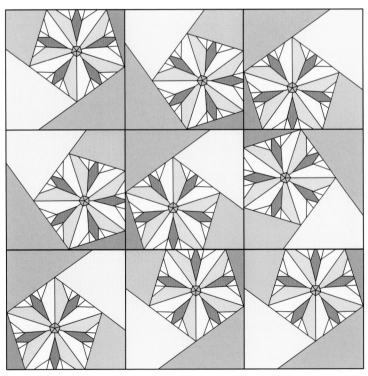

Make nine blocks.

Adding wedges to the regular pentagons to make squares is another possibility.

If the blocks are spaced in a looser organization, with squares and rectangles of various sizes, a more unusual set is possible. A quilt of this type can be planned at small scale on graph paper, with the sizes of the rectangles to be added, which are calculated from the size of the blocks. Or, the quilt can be drawn full size, and the drawing cut up to produce patterns for the pieces of the background.

Four square or rectangular St. Johnswort blocks, set in a Pinwheel around a central square. Make four blocks, then set the blocks together.

Irregular arrangement of square or rectangular St. Johnswort blocks. Make six blocks, then set the blocks together with rectangles.

In many full-size drawings of this complexity, you may find some "puzzle" pieces, which will require sewing partial seams, adding more sections, and finishing the partial seams (as shown on pages 34-35). Or you could move some seams slightly or extend one rather than another to make a pattern with no puzzle pieces (no partial seams). Consider all the options before deciding which one you prefer.

Four curved seam blocks. Make four blocks. Set the pieced blocks into large background pieces.

The pieced flowers can be used as the basis of a full-size quilting. The block edges have been erased, and the seamlines in the blocks extended as needed to make a piecing design. You will have to make the drawing for this quilt full size; that is, the size at which you intend to sew.

Or, use combinations of other views of the St. Johnswort flower; try a complete pieced plant, bud, seed head, or a single, greatly enlarged flower quilt. I'm sure you can come up with other possibilities as well. Each design will depict the St. Johnswort in a slightly different way and will have a different visual impact.

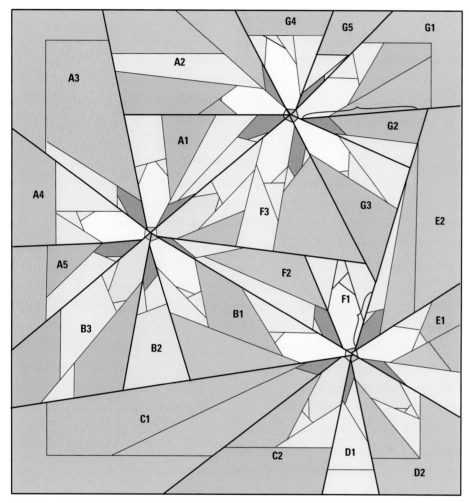

St. Johnswort quilt

Each piece of the drawing will be used once as a template for a single piece of fabric. Sew the wedges. Sew A1 to A2 to A3 to A4 to A5; sew B1 to B2 to B3; then C1 to C2; D1 to D2; E1 to E2; and sew F1 to F2 to F3. Sew partial seam 1 starting at the center of the flower, G1 to G2, stopping the seam about 1 inch from the end of G2. Sew G3 to G1G2; sew G4 to G5; and sew G4G5 to G1G2G3. Sew B to C to D. Sew partial seam 2 starting at the center of the flower, E to F, stopping the seam about 1 inch from the end of F1. Sew BCD to EF to A; add G to AF; then finish partial seam 2, E to F1G3G2. Finish partial seam 1, G1 to G2E2.

Grizzly Bears

The St. Johnswort flower had a simple radial structure that could be exploited in wedges to set up the piecing. Other images will have less clearly defined patterns that require more fiddling, compromises, and abstractions to translate them into piecework.

A photo of a mother grizzly bear and cubs was the basis for this outline drawing. Looking at the drawing carefully, and thinking about the piecing process, led me to focus first on the ruffs of fur around the mother bear's face.

Outline drawing of a mother grizzly and two cubs

seam 1

seam 2   seam 3

seam 4   seam 5

Traditional Log Cabin block and assembly process

A traditional pieced block that is familiar to most quilters is called the Log Cabin. It begins with a center square, around which are sewn "logs" of rectangles of progressively longer lengths (also see page 9).

Many contemporary versions of the Log Cabin quilt use centers of various shapes, and logs of varying sizes, to make quilts assembled in the traditional Log Cabin manner, but with different visual results.

Some contemporary Log Cabin block variations

The way the bear's head is surrounded by fur suggested a Log Cabin block approach for the piecing. The most detailed areas of the drawing are the three bear faces. The structure of the bodies is almost obscured by the masses of fur.

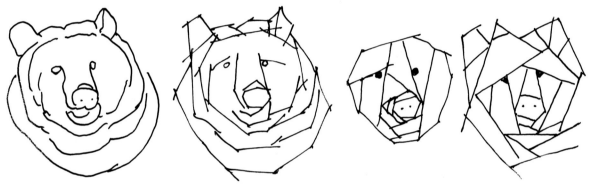

Initial sketches of mother bear's head to see if the Log Cabin method would work. Adjustments, manipulations, and erasures eventually led to a good working design.

Based on the outline drawing, I began some experimental sketches to see if I could piece first the mother bear's nose and chin, then the surrounding ruffs of fur, the eyes, and the ears.

Working sketch of mother bear for piecing

In working out the body of the bear, I am trying to suggest both the ruffs of fur and the underlying structure of the bear's skeleton. Moving the angles of some lines just slightly could make a line suggest both a ruff and the bear's shoulder. This is a tricky process. As you get more experience, you will find it gets a little easier to know which line choices to make. In addition to trying to make the bear look like a bear, you are also trying to make something you can sew reasonably well.

Adding the cubs to the drawing

Let's break the drawing down and see if we can piece it in a logical order.

Sectioning of the drawing into logical sewing pieces reveals two puzzle pieces in the mother bear's leg

I have removed both puzzle pieces by a slight redesign of the drawing. The bears can now be sewn with simple straight seams in a logical order. Rather than standing the bears on a straight line, I have taken advantage of the piecing lines from the bears to make a rough line of tundra at the bottom edge.

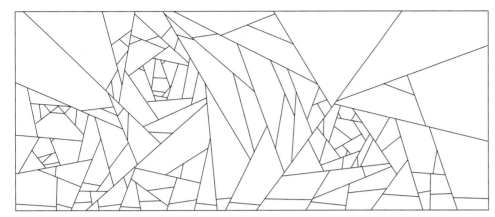

Final line drawing for the Grizzly Bears quilt

I think, if it were me, I would enlarge this drawing to about four feet wide and piece a single image rather than making repeated images, perhaps working in a suggestion of a background and an irregular border. The scale of four feet would make the pieces of fabric a comfortable size to work with and feels about right for the complexity of the drawing. The smallest patches in the design are the bears' eyes.

If I wanted a larger image, I would probably make a slightly more detailed piecing diagram. Although I might be able to sew this image at a smaller scale, such as an 18" width, the tiny size of those pieces seem too small for a grizzly bear. There is a sense of scale that I find a little hard to define between piecing that seems "quilt-like" or appropriate for the pieced quilt medium, and piecing that is so small that the individual pieces do not read as fabric patches, but rather as embroidery.

It is certainly true that I feel the need to use a range of scales of pieces in my quilting. If I use tiny pieces in part of the design, I use a bigger scale of pieces to complement them. Most traditional quilt blocks with tiny pieces (for instance, Feathered Star) use alternate uncut squares or other large patches as part of the overall design.

Assembly of Three Grizzly Bears

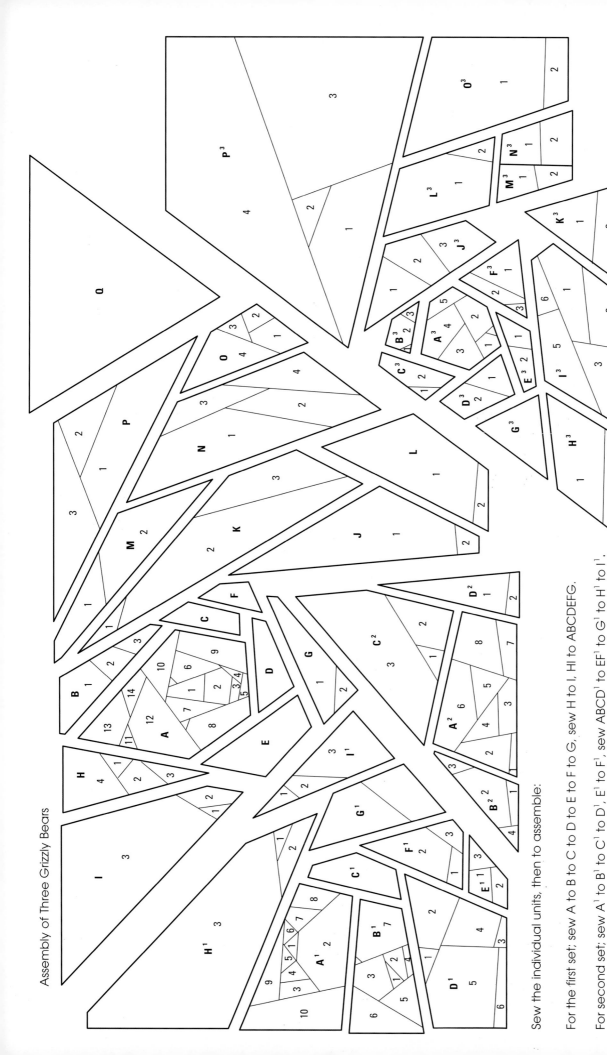

Sew the individual units, then to assemble:

For the first set; sew A to B to C to D to E to F to G, sew H to I, HI to ABCDEFG.

For second set; sew A¹ to B¹ to C¹ to D¹, E¹ to F¹, sew ABCD¹ to EF¹ to G¹ to H¹ to I¹.

For the third set; sew A² to B² to C² to D².

For the fourth set; sew ABCDEFGHI to ABCDEFGHI¹, add ABCD², add J, add K, add L, add M, add N, add O, add P, add Q.

For the fifth set; sew A³ to B³ to C³ to D³ to E³ to F³ to G³, sew H³ to I³ to ABCDEFG³, add J³, add K³, sew M³ to N³ to L³ to O³, sew ABCDEFGHIJK³ to LMNO³ to P³. Sew the two sections together.

Three Grizzly Bears
1997, 30" x 50"
machine pieced,
machine quilted, cottons
and silk, cotton batting,
(artist's collection)

Landscapes

Constructing landscapes in patchwork can be fun, but can also be very frustrating. If landscapes are seen as progressively distant layers of objects, they work fairly well as long as the layers are of solid objects. Tree trunks, houses, hills and mountains, lakes, rivers, and oceans can be suggested with fabrics. Semitransparent layers of foliage or branches, however, are much more difficult to achieve with fabric. A degree of abstraction is certainly forced by the concept of trying to represent three-dimensional space on a two-dimensional plane, as well as by the medium of fabric to represent stones and water.

Subtle shadings can sometimes be suggested by the use of shaded fabrics or by carefully selecting adjacent prints so that their printed designs blend into each other and disguise a seam. Depth can be suggested by using larger scale patterns in the foreground and smaller patterns or solids further back, or by using crisp definite patterns in the foreground and subtle patterns or wrong sides for the distance.

However, because of the limits of working with piecing, most seams are necessarily straight or gently curved. It is extremely difficult to piece a very irregular or angular edge. In some situations, hand or machine appliqué may be useful.

Fabric selections for landscapes usually require different choices of colors, textures, and patterns than are used most often in traditional quilting. Study the colors and textures outside your window or in a favorite photograph. Grays, mustards, dull greens and bright greens, purples, blacks, browns, and many mixtures of colors may have to be added to your fabric stash. A variety of values of all of those colors (dark darks, mediums, light lights, and mixtures of values dark/light, medium/light, and medium/dark) as well as a variety of scales and types of prints and plaids will prove helpful.

Indeed, many times choosing a fabric of the proper value, whether green or blue or brown, will be more important than the actual hue.

WORKING FROM A PHOTOGRAPH

Beginning to design a quilt from a landscape can be an intimidating process. Some students feel comfortable, pencil in hand, to sketch out a drawing from which to work. Other students, often with little drawing experience, find it helpful to begin with a tracing from a photograph.

In translating landscape into the piecing medium, a great deal of abstraction is necessary. The photograph itself is an abstract, a flat surface of colors on paper representing three-dimensional space and Mother Nature. In moving from a photograph to a quilt, many details will have to be eliminated, and others only implied. Of course, in designing the quilt, there is a lot of freedom as well for the quiltmaker to cut down trees, move mountains, eliminate telephone poles, and change the seasons of the year. Or to combine several photos from different points of view or from different time periods.

The photo tracing is simply a time saver, a place to begin the process. As I have worked on quilts over the years, my drawing skills have markedly improved. The photos, if I still use any, are there for reference, while the drawings come more and more from my hand and arm.

HORN POND

I chose the photograph of the alley of trees at Horn Pond as a starting place because the scene was rather simple in organization. The trees are almost evenly spaced and about the same size. The road is vanishing in the distance. The little figure makes a good focal point to emphasize the one-point perspective.

Photograph of a road lined with trees. Horn Pond, Woburn, Massachusetts

Tracing the contours
and edges of the Horn
Pond photograph

As I drew in the branches that canopy the roadway, oak trees for the most part, I found that they seemed to make a network of lines. The oak branches interlace over the path at very similar angles. Although the road is basically straight, it undulates very slightly and the edges are obscured with drifts of leaves. The land behind the trees on the right slopes up slightly, fading into brush and saplings.

This simplified version would not be difficult to sew. Very few lines are more than slight-ly curved. Horizontal lines cross the road and bend up slightly on either side to form a base for the tree trunks. A linear pattern like a small plaid with some light in it could be cut and pieced at different angles in the areas between the branches. The linear pattern of the plaid would suggest the small branches and twigs that almost obscure the sky.

Simplified drawing of Horn Pond with free-hand straightish lines

Horn Pond 1, from drawing,

1997, 43" x 55.5"

machine pieced,

machine quilted, cottons,

cotton batting

(artist's collection)

Fabric choices will have a great influence on the visual result of the quilt. A landscape of solids looks very crisp and modern. Yet, the whole scene can change dramatically with wild prints or plaids or batiks.

Straight-line piecing diagram for *Horn Pond 2* developed from the drawing

I have made small quilt examples from several of the diagrams from Horn Pond, enlarging the diagrams on a copier. Working on tracing paper over the drawing and using a short ruler, I've developed a straight-seam piecing diagram. The piecing starts in the center with the section labeled A. (The figure in this quilt was hand appliquéd. Nobody said it was quilt in a day.)

Sew A1 to A2 to A3 to A4 to A5. Add A6, then A7, A8, A9, A10, A11, and A12. Sew A13 to A14 and join to A12. Continue, making sections B, C, D, E, and add them in order to A. Sew F1 to F2, and add to ABCDE. Sew F3 to F4; F5 to F6; F7 to F8; and add them to ABCDEF as well. Sew section G (trunk plus four slivers), then sections H, I, J, K, L, M, N, O P, Q, R, S, T, U, V, W, X, and add them progressively to the center. Join Y1, Y2, Y3, Y4. Then sew to the part of the seam joining Y4 to R5, R6, R7, R8. Add Y5, and add Y6. Sew Z1,2,3,4,5. Sew Z6,7,8 and add to Z1,2,3,4,5 unit, then add Z9. Sew AA1,2,3, then sections BB, CC, DD, EE, FF. Join AA to Z to Y. Join BB to CC. Then add BBCC unit to AAZY unit. Add DD. Finish sewing seam joining YZD to the center. Sew EE to FF and add to the rest. Sew GG. Sew HH to GG13,14 seam, starting at the trunk W1 and leaving the seam partially open. Sew GGHH to center. Sew II1,2,3,4. Add to center. Add tree trunk II5. Sew JJ1,2. Sew KK 1 to 2 to 3, KK4 to 5, to KK1,2,3, add KK 6,7,8. Sew LL, Sew MM. Sew NN 1,2...15. Join JJ to KK to LL to MM to NN, to II5. Add NN16,17. Sew OO and add to the rest. Sew PP 1,2,3,4,5 and add to scene. Sew seam joining PP6 to HH, PP1,2. Finish seam between PP6 and GG13. Sew QQ and RR and add to the rest and you are done!

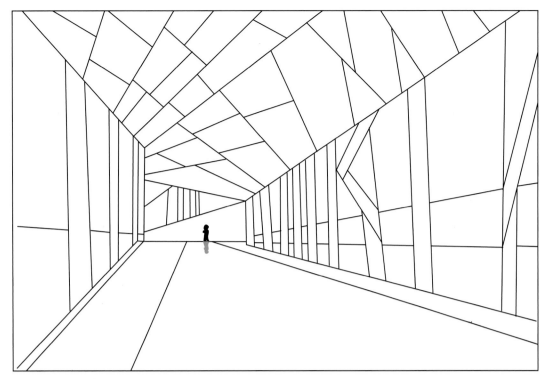

Abstract version of Horn Pond

A naturalistic landscape can also be the starting point for a more abstract treatment. The straight-line drawing looks like architecture or a stage set.

Horn Pond 3

1997, 37" x 49"

machine pieced,

machine quilted,

cottons, cotton batting

(artist's collection)

Horn Pond 4

1997, 37" x 49"

machine pieced,

machine quilted,

cottons, cotton batting

(artist's collection)

Each version treats the landscape in a different way, although I have tried to keep the colors somewhat similar from quilt to quilt.

MUIR WOODS

Bright highlights and dark shadows play an important part in this forest landscape. A lacy foliage canopy is one of the hardest things to sew effectively in patchwork. There are very dark areas here, and also very light ones. However, the light areas are mottled mixtures and include small amounts of medium and dark tones as well. There are also medium areas, mottled with light and dark, and dark areas with a few light highlights.

Photograph of

Redwoods,

Muir Woods, California

You will need a collection of fabrics for the mottled leaves, some about 80% light, some 60% light, some 40% light, and some 20% light, in medium-scale prints if possible. Although the colors in the photo are mainly yellows, greens, browns, and blacks, finding the right amount of highlights and mottling is more important to creating the feeling of this grove than finding the right hue. Unlike the previous example, there are few clear contour edge lines, but lots of areas of dappled foliage.

Careful tracing from Muir Woods photograph

Angular piecing, mostly short seams and inset corners

I've developed an angular sketch with the strong vertical lines of the trunks and horizontal piecing of the forest floor. The area of foliage is broken into chunks from the differing amounts of mottled highlights present in the variety of fabrics. Piecing from this diagram is complicated, but possible, with lots of short seams and inset corners.

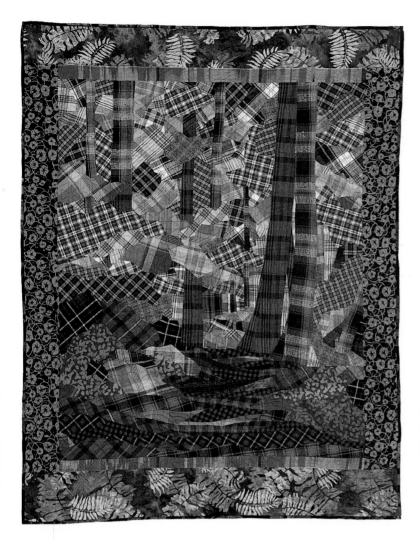

Muir Woods 1

1997, 49.5" x 38"

machine pieced,

machine quilted,

cottons, cotton batting

(artist's collection)

Enlarging the sketch, I was able to construct *Muir Woods 1*, using many small plaids for the lacy foliage.

Let's see what happens if I try to simplify the sketch to make it easier to sew. Enlarging the sketch on a copier to 400%, a size that felt comfortable to sew, I began by pinning the enlarged drawing on the design wall. In this case, I used a letter to indicate each section and a number to indicate the sewing order, and numbered and lettered each piece in the drawing. For the template drawing, I copied the enlargement of the figure onto the shiny side of freezer paper, using a fine-tipped permanent marker. I marked the light areas with capital L's.

Following the directions in the Piecing Complicated Quilts section, I set about constructing *Muir Woods 2*.

Auditioning fabrics for

Muir Woods 2

Sew sections A, B, C, D, E, F, G. Join B to C, A to D to E, and F to G. Join ADE to BC. Sew FG to C, leaving the seam open at the left side. Add P1, then P2, then P3, and P4. Sew sections H, I, J, K, M, N, O, Q, R. Sew R to S to Q to P. Add H. Sew I to O, then add to rest. Add J to I, then to HF, then finish the seam at C. Sew K to JI. Sew K to O. Sew M to N, and add to the rest.

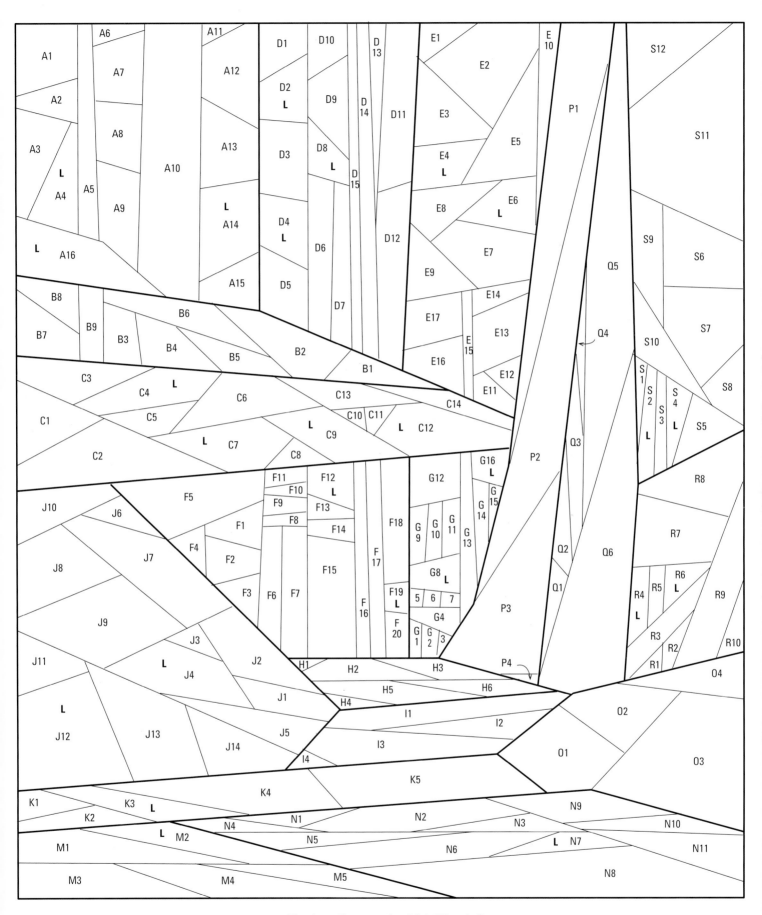

Piecing diagram for *Muir Woods 2*

Stage 1

Stage 2

As fabric selections are made, templates are cut from the full-size freezer-paper drawing. Each piece of freezer paper was ironed onto the wrong side of the selected fabric. Using a pencil, I traced around the edge of the paper template onto the fabric, and marked any tics. With the template stuck to the fabric, I cut the fabric piece, leaving a ¼" seam allowance outside the edge of the freezer paper. The cut fabric piece, with the paper template attached, was then pinned onto the drawing on the wall. As fabric selections are made, the photograph from which I began became less important with the growing quilt influencing fabric choices more and more. The fabrics start a dialogue and the literal photographic landscape is put aside.

Stage 3

Stage 4

Muir Woods 2

pieced top, unbordered

Muir Woods 2

1997, 46" x 40"

machine pieced,

machine quilted,

cottons, cotton batting

(artist's collection)

With the pieced top pinned to the design wall, I began to consider what border I wanted to add, if any. Auditioning various fabrics, then selecting those that balanced and refined the composition and colors of the top and framed the piece without confining it, I arrived at the finished top. Quilting was done by machine free-motion, using cotton thread.

Smooth curve pieced with short seams and Y's, Muir Woods

I've made another drawing of Muir Woods at a level of complexity similar to *Muir Woods 2*, but with smooth curves this time. Although I haven't yet made this version in fabric, the cartoon quality of the smooth curves in the drawing does not appeal to me as much as the angularity of the drawing of *Muir Woods 1* and *Muir Woods 2.*

Photograph of water-worn rocks and pot-holes in the Deerfield River at Shelburne Falls, Massachusetts

POTHOLES AT SHELBURNE FALLS

The last landscape photo I will work from is of some water-worn rocks and potholes in the Deerfield River at Shelburne Falls, Massachusetts.

Rather than foliage, this photo is primarily of rocks and small pools of water, with very light areas and very dark areas. Foliage is confined to the lower left corner. This image is a very different kind of landscape than the Horn Pond grove or Muir Woods.

Careful tracing of the contours and areas of light and dark in the Shelburne Falls Potholes

Angular piecing drawing for *Potholes 1*

The angular piecing diagram is not very far removed from the tracing. The textures of the rocks and some of the lights, cracks, and shadows can be suggested with the fabrics selected as well as with piecing.

Two other aspects of the scene, the reflectivity of the pools and the cluster of greenery in the deep pothole in the lower left corner, are also elements that I will try to suggest with the fabrics chosen.

I made *Potholes 1* from this drawing. In selecting a size to use, I was guided both by the size of the smallest pieces in my diagram and by the feeling of the photograph. In this case, I enlarged the drawing to 42.5" by 31". That made the narrowest slivers of fabric about ½" wide.

Auditioning fabrics for *Potholes 1*

Stage 1

Stage 2

As with the *Muir Woods 2* sequence, the full-size drawing was traced on the shiny side of freezer paper. The original enlarged drawing was pinned to the design wall with the freezer-paper template drawing on top of it. Piece by piece the freezer-paper drawing was cut and ironed onto the wrong side of the selected fabric. A pencil line traced onto the wrong side of the fabric around the edge of the freezer paper will mark the seamline. Add tic marks and cut the fabric pieces with a ¼" seam allowance. Because of the curved seams and inset corners in this quilt, the freezer-paper pieces must be removed from the back of the fabric pieces before the sewing is begun. Remove each paper as you get to it.

Stage 3

Stage 4

Potholes 1 pieced top, unbordered

Potholes 1

1997, 53" x 42"

machine pieced,

machine quilted,

cottons, cotton batting

(artist's collection)

Beginning to straighten the seams in *Potholes 1*

Potholes 1 contains some very complex piecing, but maintains much of the character of the rocks. As an experiment to simplify construction, I made another drawing with straight lines, *Potholes 2*. On another piece of tracing paper over the *Potholes 1* diagram, I began to try to straighten some of the seams.

This diagram, with straight seams, is somewhat easier to piece than the earlier piecing drawing (on page 137), but does contain many inset corners, Y seams, and puzzle pieces. Given those difficulties, I prefer the character of *Potholes 1* to this straight-seam version.

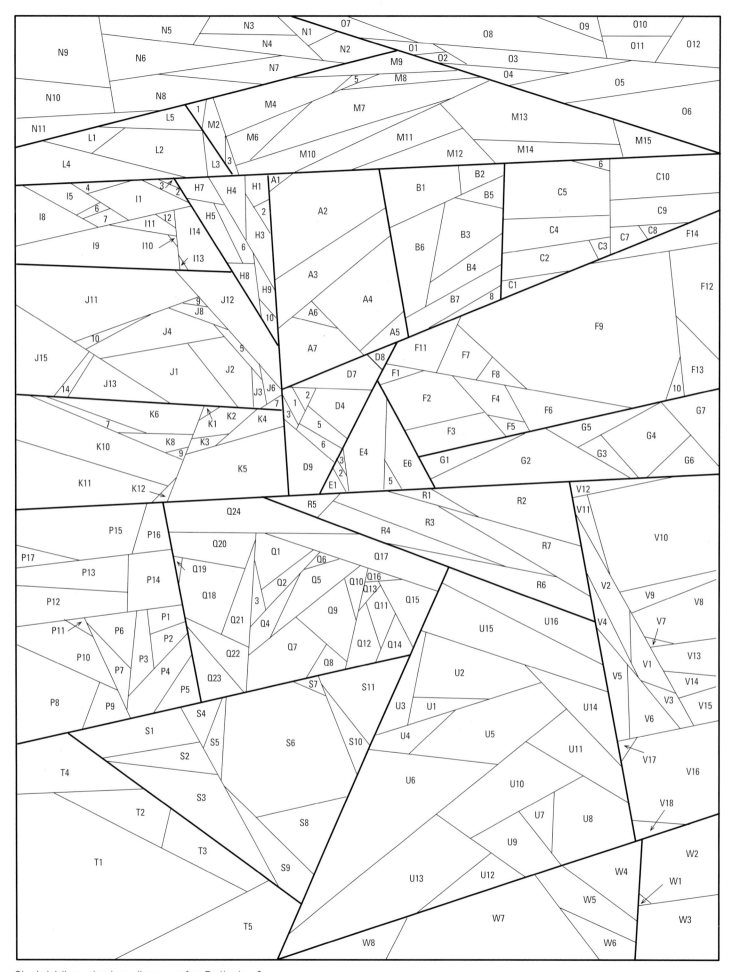

Straight-line piecing diagram for *Potholes 3*

Further work on yet another piece of tracing paper led to a diagram which can be pieced in sections with straight seams.

In this version the technical sewing problems have been resolved. The diagram can be pieced in sections A to W, sewing each section in the numbered order.

Join the sections by sewing A to B to C, G to F to E to D, I to J to K to H, L to M to N to O. Then join ABC to DEFG, add HIJK, and LMNO to complete the top half. Join P to Q, and S to T. Sew PQ to ST. Add U. Add R. Add V. Add W. Then sew the top and bottom halves together.

The straight seams are angles that approximate the curves of the rocks. The great many pieces allow for many different fabrics and values to be used to show off the forms of the potholes. Indicate on the enlarged drawing where the darks and lights will be to help keep it oriented to the photograph.

The lines of a landscape may suggest quite an abstract composition, one in which the natural features are no longer the focus. The shape of the curves in the rock is quite wonderful, and, greatly simplified, led to the diagram for *Potholes 4*.

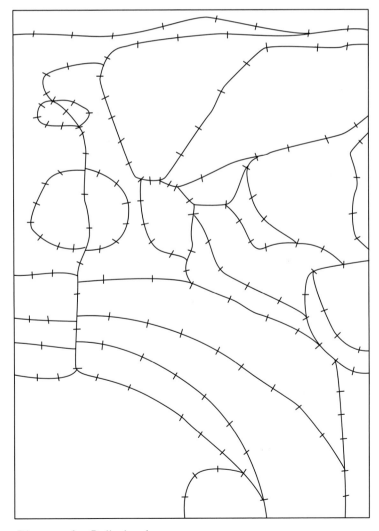

Diagram for *Potholes 4*

Potholes 4

1997, 48" x 39.5"

machine pieced,

machine quilted, cottons,

cotton batting

(artist's collection)

The fabric selection for my version of *Potholes 4* began with a brown, blue, and lavender African print from a friend, then went on to include other African fabrics, some Marimekko® screen-printed fabrics from Finland, and a few contemporary quilt cottons. A border was added as needed, and free-motion machine quilting was done with a dark cotton thread.

With the three landscape photographs as examples, I've made several distinctly different versions of quilts, varying in degree of abstraction as well as in methods of construction and fabric choices. I hope they will give you an impetus to try your own version.

Finding Your Working Style

Every serious quiltmaker I know gradually develops a method of working that is comfortable for her or him. The method I use, involving complicated drawings and piecing from paper templates, is one that works well for me. Some students find it comfortable for them as well.

This method requires concentrated attention to detail in drawing, planning, fabric selection, and precision piecing. Some students find this hard to manage in the confusion of a workshop setting, and are much more comfortable in their own space when they can find some uninterrupted time. Some find it hard to do the drawing, or have trouble getting from the drawing into fabric choices. Some find the careful planning and piecing frustrating. Many prefer a quicker and more spontaneous assembly method. On the otherhand, many students find this method works for them as well and gives them the freedom use almost any imagery that appeals to them.

There are many other ways of making quilts. Find a method that is comfortable for you and allows you to make the quilts you want to create.

The Western Sea
1995, 34.5″ x 43″
machine pieced,
machine appliquéd,
machine quilted,
cottons, cotton batting
(private collection)

Fabric Selection

SELECTING FABRICS

There are at least as many ways of selecting fabrics and using them in quilts as there are quiltmakers. Just as you found a style and method of working, you must now experiment with pattern and scale, plaids and prints, lights and darks, and degrees of contrast to find the ones that work for you.

This is a process that will take both time and experience. It will help to expand your usual fabric choices if you acquire some unusual ones and try to begin using them.

Detail of *The Western Sea*, shown on page 145

A rather naturalistic landscape, *The Western Sea*, was pieced with rocks of various cottons, a piece of a particular hand-dye, and a piece of drapery fabric with a very light sky with the suggestion of a glowing sun. In studying the quilt top, my eye caught a piece of Chinese batik, pale orange with white and dark blue, and a very strange pattern. I suppose the large white polka dots on blue in the batik reminded me of the small white dots on one of the rock fabrics. Anyway, a big piece of the batik arrived in the quilt. It's much more interesting to look at and creates a lot of wonder at shows: "What is that thing in the sky?" I don't know. It just happened. Maybe it's the Loch Ness monster on the California coast.

For the most part, students have more bright colors and dark to medium fabrics than they may need, but not enough subtle shades and mixtures, large scale fabrics, and light fabrics. This is partly the seduction of the fabric store at work. In a vast array of color, it is hard to choose to buy pale and subtle fabrics.

Detail of *Cape Ann Calm*

A white and blue large-scale brush stroke print (used wrong side up in *Cape Ann Calm*) was intended by me to represent a bank of clouds in the sky at Rockport, Massachusetts. Nancy Halpern saw them as the Alps at Lake Como, and I've heard they are also glaciered mountains at Homer, Alaska. This seems to be a universal coast, in fact.

The clump of grass at the lower left is pieced from a black background, gold-grass batik. The grass was printed in blocks. I had to join several blocks together at slight angles to get a clump the size I wanted. Using a much darker value blue in the sea, right above the grass, masks the edge of the clump feathery. It blends with the black batik background. A lighter blue here would have made the seam between the black batik and the sea above it much more prominent.

I like very much how the trees at the top of the point of land work with the light sky. The trees are mostly part of a border of a batik skirt given to me by a clever quilter. The little black lines seem to be trunks and branches. The white dots and ochre are close to the same value as the sky. I've also included little bits of a marbleized fabric—the edge where a large area of purple met a light blue. This adds the suggestion of another layer of tree-tops. Large scale unusual prints are usually notoriously poor sellers, and it takes a brave and independent shop owner to take the chances to stock a few.

Cape Ann Calm
1997, 37.5" x 52.5"
machine pieced,
machine quilted,
cottons, cotton batting
(private collection)

The Guitar

1996, 36" x 46"

machine pieced,

hand appliquéd,

machine quilted,

cottons, cotton batting

(private collection)

Fabric choices for *The Guitar* started with the red and green African print used for the child's shirt. The bright golds in that print were picked up by the gold plaid for the guitar and by the small Nine-Patches on purple in the background fabric (one I designed myself). As the quilt developed, the Nine-Patches seemed like bits of music. A few more of them are appliquéd in additional places.

Actually, the fabric I chose for the musician's hair and mustache are almost the same value as this purple fabric. To keep the mustache from disappearing into the purple, I appliquéd a small Nine-Patch block just under that part of the profile.

The white fabric with fruit is a piece of an antique feedsack. Notice that the cut and resewn plaid in the shirt suggests the shape of the musician. The radishes, a fabric from a friend in Switzerland, was the right scale of print, and the colors and contrasted values that I needed to finish the border. Maybe the shape of the radishes also suggests the shape of a musical note.

Knowing all this, I try to search out the fabrics I need first, poking in corners, and carefully studying for unusual lights, before I let myself be drawn to the bright fabrics demanding attention. This can take considerable willpower. I also look at dress and shirting fabrics, furnishing fabrics, antique fabrics, and for recycling possibilities at rummage sales and used clothing shops.

Interesting lights are hard to find, especially those with bits of other colors in them. The white smoke ring fabric in the sky is one of my own design. The blues are the right and wrong sides of an apron from a rummage sale. Cutting the sky into swoops makes a nice design; it also made pieces that fit the fabric scraps I had to work with.

Study quilts that especially appeal to you to discover precisely what fabrics are being used. Write notes if necessary. Focus on the individual fabrics, including the light ones, and the percentages of each in the quilt. Try to find something similar, even if you are not sure how to use it at the time.

Seascape with Iceplant
1993, 33" x 77.5"
machine pieced,
machine quilted, cottons,
cotton batting
(private collection)

From Point Bonita
1989, 36" x 46"
machine pieced, hand
appliquéd, machine
quilted, cottons,
cotton batting
(private collection)

The sand and borders of this quilt are drapery fabrics, as is the streaky fabric in the clay cliffs. Like the mountain in *Aurora*, on page 150, using this type fabric rather than piecing small bits keeps the cliffs from being too fussy and detracting from the details of the sea edge and buildings.

Aurora

1996, 35" x 44"

machine pieced,

machine quilted,

cottons, cotton batting

(private collection).

BUILDING A STASH

You will probably also find that you will want to develop a stash of your own, rather than depending on your local fabric supplier to have just the right thing available.

The sky is a single half-yard piece of a hand-dyed fabric, in a way, a "cheater" cloth. I'd often speculate about how one could depict the aurora borealis in fabric. As soon as I saw this piece, I knew I had found it.

This small quilt is made with only 13 different fabrics. The larger mountain is a single fabric, shaded dark and light. Using a paint-by-number fracturing technique to piece the lights and darks of a mountain such as this one makes it overly fussy. People focus on all the little bits of fabric, rather than the mass of the mountain. I wanted a very loose transition from the top of the line of trees to the foothills, and found a drapery print with black and white dots. The seamline between the lacy tops of the trees and the foothills is now almost invisible because of that fabric choice. Blending fabrics like this is impossible to do if you use only solid fabrics.

The stash is as individual as the quiltmaker. Some are confined to a single bag or basket. Some have expanded to fill entire rooms and whole buildings.

MYTHICAL FABRICS

However big the stash, it will never contain every fabric that you imagine you need. Or enough of every fabric so that you never run out in the middle of a project.

What to use for the bark of the largest tree trunk in *A Carpet of Goldthread* was a real problem. I didn't like anything I had (and, of course, couldn't find anything suitable in my

A Carpet of Goldthread
1988, 62" x 107"
machine pieced, hand
appliquéd, hand quilted,
cottons, blends, linens,
rayon, permanent ink,
polyester batting
(private collection)

Canada Mayflowers
1993, 39" x 43"
machine pieced,
machine quilted, cot-
tons, mother-of-pearl
buttons, cotton batting
(private collection)

local fabric stores). I used a shaded (light to dark) piece of brown drapery fabric, and drew the black line pattern of the bark with a permanent marker, then appliquéd some highlights and quilted along the black cracks with purple thread. I've invented mythical fabrics by the score, "If I could only find something like that, but with mustard and orange, and a little black dot, and some flecks of light, and with a little glaze to the finish." Of course, mythical fabrics don't exist.

The foamy white blossoms in *Canada Mayflowers* are a sign of spring in New England. I went to great lengths here to keep the airiness of the foam. Pieced under the blossoms is a white and black batik with irregular polka dots. The black matches the value of the fabrics used in the backgrounds. White cotton thread in free-motion quilting was then used to draw stars on the batik. Mother-of-pearl buttons sewn to the surface with big stitches complete the flowers and add bright highlights.

REASSESS WHAT YOU HAVE

Use what fabric you have, but try to look at your fabrics in different ways. Consider using the wrong side of fabrics. Cut up and re-sew at angles a dominant stripe or plaid to subdue it to your will.

It was difficult to find the kind of purples I wanted for the Jacaranda blossoms. One fabric that did work was a plaid. I have cut and re-sewn the plaid in the area under the tree to represent the fallen blooms. If I had used the plaid in a larger piece here, the straight lines of the plaid would have overwhelmed the quilt. Fracturing and re-sewing allows the lines to bend.

If you run out of a fabric before you finish a quilt, and revise your original plan by finding something else to add, almost always a more interesting quilt results.

Jacaranda Tree

1996, 39" x 45"

machine pieced,

machine quilted,

cottons,

cotton batting

(private collection)

Light and Shadow

1989, 56.5" x 31"

machine pieced, hand

appliquéd, machine

quilted, cottons, linen,

cotton blends,

cotton batting

(private collection)

Wood, Rocks, and Water

1995, 42.5" x 61"

machine pieced,

machine appliquéd,

machine quilted, cottons,

cotton batting

(private collection)

FINDING FABRICS SPECIFICALLY FOR NATURE QUILTS

Endeavoring to use references to the natural world in your quilts can complicate the already difficult design, composition, and color issues that encumber the making of any quilt. To me, the different aspects of light are a crucial factor. In translating a natural image to a fabric surface, one of the most difficult issues to deal with using available fabrics is the depiction or indication of the infinite variety of light and shadow.

Very light fabrics, medium fabrics, and dark fabrics in a variety of colors are readily available in solids or in the mini-prints that visually might as well be solids. What is generally lacking are prints that contain lights and darks, or lights and mediums, in a variety of different ratios and scales. The edges of the shadows are sharply defined here by the adjacent light and dark fabrics.

Compare the diffused shadows in *Wood Rocks and Water* with *Light and Shadow*. A very lacy tree at the left has small soft-edge appliquéd scraps added to the surface. This is especially hard to deal with in trying to depict different densities of foliage against a sky, or in scattered bright highlights in an area that is primarily medium to dark.

Maine Woods

1991, 76" x 76.5"

machine pieced,

hand appliquéd,

machine quilted, cottons,

cotton batting

(private collection)

Photo by Carina Woolrich

From the Lookout

1994, 24.5" x 69"

machine pieced,

machine appliquéd,

machine quilted, cot-

tons, cotton batting

(private collection)

Plaids

Plaids for quilting, shirting, clothing, and furnishing fabrics can often help solve some of the problems with light. They often contain very varied and interesting combinations of values and colors. The grid structure of plaids also replicates in miniature the grid structure in traditional patchwork, acting almost like miniature quilts.

The grid structure of plaids can also be used to imply architecture or man-made objects. Plaids used off-grain and turned at angles away from true vertical can be easily read as landscape, trees, rocks, or other natural objects. Plaids used with one grain precisely vertical read as buildings or objects made by man.

On the lower border of this plaid landscape, *From the Lookout,* I've added soft-edge appliqué houses and barns, cutting each from a plaid or stripe aligned vertically. Because the lower border is also composed of plaid squares aligned vertically, it usually takes a while for the viewer to notice the buildings.

Verena's Lily

1993, 51" x 33.5"

machine pieced,

machine quilted,

cottons, linens,

cotton batting

(private collection)

Novelty Nature Prints

There have been many fabrics manufactured recently to solve some of the difficulties in translating nature into fabric quilts. You can find ranges of mountains, groves of trees, pebbles, waves, icebergs, grizzly bears, wood grain, sky, and clouds printed "realistically" by the yard.

Probably because of my contrary nature, I can't stand to use most of these. Or at least to use them as their designers intended. I'd rather use plaids and prints, or florals and geometrics, to suggest natural images in my quilts, and use printed pebbles for herds of walrus, clouds for waterfalls, or icebergs for lilies. Of course, other choices are equally valid.

Freesias 2
1994, 51" x 42"
machine pieced, hand
appliquéd, machine
quilted, cottons,
cotton batting
(private collection)

Most quilters are fabric lovers. They need to touch the fabrics in a store before buying them. Folding and unfolding, washing and pressing, cutting and sewing, and finally quilting are all very important tactile parts of working in this medium. Although quilters' reactions to the materials are similar, their fabric choices are as individual as the quilters making them. The collecting of fabrics into a quilt can be a collaboration between the artist and the piece. Let the fabrics talk to you. Be willing to listen.

Foxgloves II
1983, 39" x 62"
machine pieced,
hand quilted, cottons,
blends, poly batting
(artist's collection)

Conclusion

This book has come directly from my own work with nearly 300 quilts over the past twenty-five years, and from my own experiences with students and as a teacher all over the world. It has been a continuous, and tremendously exciting, learning and exploring process for me. Perspectives change over time and my perception changes with them. Every quilt is a step along the way. I hope you have enjoyed this journey through the patchwork medium with me, and that *Piecing: Expanding the Basics* stimulates your own involvement with patchwork and quilts.

About the Author

Ruth B. McDowell is an internationally known professional quilt artist, teacher, lecturer, and author. She has made over 250 quilts during the last two decades. Her quilts have been seen in several solo shows, as well as in dozens of magazines and books. Her previous books include Symmetry, and the first book in C&T Publishing's Art & Inspirations series, which provides an in-depth look at her outstanding career. Ruth resides in Winchester, Massachusetts.

Bibliography

Grunbaum, Branko and Shepard, G. C. *Tilings and Patterns*, W H Freeman: New York, 1986

Malcolm, Bill and Nancy. *New Zealand Alpine Plants, Inside and Out.* Craig Potton: Nelson, New Zealand, 1988

Walters, Anna Lee. *The Spirit of Native America*; grizzly bear photograph by Tom and Pat Leeson (page 32). Chronicle Books: San Francisco, 1989.

Index

For more information write
for a free catalog:
C&T Publishing, Inc.
P.O. Box 1456
Lafayette, CA 94549
(800) 284-1114
http://www.ctpub.com
e-mail: ctinfo@ctpub.com

For quilting supplies:
Cotton Patch Mail Order
3405 Hall Lane, Dept. CTB
Lafayette, CA 94549
e-mail: cottonpa@aol.com
(800) 835-4418
(510) 283-7883